Exchange
Rate and
Foreign
Exchange
Policies
in Korea

About author

Mr. Byungchan Ahn graduated in February 1977 from the College of Political Science and Economics of Korea University with highest honors. Upon graduation, he joined the Bank of Korea and served over 34 years, retiring on 24 March 2011. He specialized in money and banking, foreign exchange, and international finance, while posted with Research Department, Monetary Policy Department, and International Department.

Mr. Ahn also received a masters degree in economics from Pennsylvania State University in May 1987 through the fellowship of the Bank of Korea. He was seconded as a visiting scholar to the Research Division of the Federal Reserve Bank of St. Louis in the United States from September 1993 to August 1994, where he conducted research on the determination of interest rate and exchange rate policies in a small open economy. When he returned to Korea, he was appointed as Chief of Monetary Management Division at the Monetary Policy Department, where he oversaw target setting and management of monetary aggregates until February 1997. He also served as Director-General of International Department from May 2007 to August 2010, a period which included the outbreak of the biggest global crisis since the Great Depression of 1930s. Most notably, he played an important role in establishing temporary swap arrangements between the Bank of Korea and the US Federal Reserve, and provisions of swap funds to domestic commercial banks. He also led the department to introduce an FX forward position limit system in cooperation with the government. Prior to becoming the head of International Department, he served two years and six months as Chief Representative of the Bank's Washington DC Representative Office, where he strengthened the institution's ties with the US Federal Reserve, the US Treasury and the International Monetary Fund. Since March 2011, he has been the chief audit officer at KB Investment & Securities in Korea.

Exchange Rate and Foreign Exchange Policies in Korea

Byungchan Ahn

hannarae

Exchange Rate and Foreign Exchange Policies in Korea
© 2013 Byungchan Ahn
Published by Hannarae Publishing Co.

Hannarae Publishing Co.
2F, Hapjeong Bldg., 39, Worldcup–ro 3gil, Hapjeong–dong, Mapo–gu,
Seoul, Republic of Korea, 121–885
t. 82–2–738–5637 | f. 82–2–363–5637
hannarae91@naver.com
www.hannarae.net

First Printing August 20, 2013
Printed in the Republic of Korea

ISBN 978–89–5566–147–7 93320

A CIP catalogue record for this book is available from the National Library of Korea (CIP2013012375)

C O N T E N T S

이 책은 방일영문화재단의 지원을 받아 저술 · 출판되었습니다.

This book was written and published with support from the Bang Il Young Foundation.

Blurb for Ahn's book

With free capital movements between countries, emerging economies are vulnerable to the ebb and flow of international investment funds. The lessons drawn from the 1997 Asian currency crisis helped Korea get through the recent global financial crisis with relatively small adverse effects on its economy. As one of the persons in charge of assessing market movements and implementing stabilization policies at the time, the author made valuable contributions to the appropriate management of the financial crisis. This book gives readers a good opportunity to grasp the practical realities of the Korean foreign exchange markets and understand the policy challenges authorities in emerging markets face in the current globalized financial system.

Lee, Seongtae

Former Governor
The Bank of Korea

This is the first book to treat comprehensively the workings of the foreign exchange market and the framework of foreign exchange policy in Korea. It is written by a former Bank of Korea senior manager who dealt extensively with policy issues and foreign exchange management for more than 30 years. Mr. Ahn has produced an excellent book by combining his practical hands-on experiences with economic theory to help the reader understand the process of Korea's capital account liberalization and the rationale behind it. He also provides detailed analyses of external debt, liquidity management and foreign exchange regulations. This is a very useful book that both academics and market practitioners should read to deepen their understanding of the actions of Korea's policymakers in maintaining foreign exchange market stability in Korea.

Park, Yung Chul

Distinguished Professor
Division of International Studies
Korea University

This is an excellent book. Unlike most of the books by foreign authors on exchange rates and FX policies, this one deals with many critical issues of FX markets from the standpoint of Korea, a small and open economy without a convertible currency. That is the most distinguishing feature of the book. As many emerging economies are inundated with foreign capital as a result of the quantitative easing policies of major central banks, it is becoming increasingly harder to find the right mix of FX policy and other macroeconomic policies such as monetary policy. Reflecting his own experiences at the Bank of Korea during the turbulent days of the global financial crisis, he vividly explains the agony and, at the same time, the creativity and ingenuity of the FX policy makers including himself. His writing style is such that a dry and complicated topic like exchange rates can be easily understood. For all those who would like to be players in the FX market and/or industry, this book is a must read.

Choi, Dosoung

Vice President for Global Advancement and Professor
Handong Global University
Former Member of the Monetary Policy Committee
The Bank of Korea

Preface

Korea experienced a severe economic recession and financial turbulence owing to a currency crisis in late-1997 and the global financial crisis in September 2008. The second time around the nation, however, was able to rapidly recover within a short period of time. In August and September 2012, three major international credit rating agencies raised Korea's sovereign credit rating. The simultaneous upgrade is virtually unparalleled in the world since the global financial crisis of 2008. Moody's Investors Service pointed out four key drivers for its rating upgrade: strong fiscal fundamentals, a high degree of economic resilience and competitiveness, the continuation of the status-quo in North-South geopolitics, and the reduced external vulnerability of the banking sector. In this and similar ways, changes in Korea's external finances have had very significant effects on the nation's economy and creditworthiness.

This book describes inner workings of Korea's exchange rate and foreign exchange policies related to the nation's external finances, specifically focusing on Korea's successful management of its foreign currency liquidity crisis in the wake of Lehman Brothers' collapse in September 2008. This English version includes recent developments and changes in the system since the original Korean edition was published on 10 May 2011. The Korean edition was selected as one of the "Outstanding Books of 2012" by Korea's National Academy of Sciences. The purpose of this book is to facilitate a better understanding of Korea's exchange rate and foreign exchange policies among a wider international audience, including institutional investors, corporate treasurers and policy makers, particularly those in emerging market economies.

Korea achieved remarkable economic development in a short period of time through the use of foreign funds to make up a shortage of domestic capital. But this exposed the country to excessive exchange rate volatility and massive capital outflows following the 1997 and 2008 currency crises. While Korea has been globally lauded for its ability to quickly overcome these events, they also highlight the role of foreign exchange policy in managing the exchange rate movements and foreign capital flows of the Korean economy, which has a high degree of external dependency and a near fully-opened capital market.

The main subject of this book is Korea's exchange rate and foreign exchange policies. While other works have confined themselves to the country's exchange rate or foreign exchange market, it is very difficult to find one that comprehensively covers all the related topics, such as foreign exchange reserves, external debt, capital market liberalization, and the prudential regulation of the foreign exchange sector. This book focuses particularly on changes in Korea's exchange rate and foreign exchange policies since the 2008 global financial crisis, as well as the policy tasks that have yet to be resolved or tackled in the coming years.

One of the reasons I first wrote this book was to share my experience and the knowledge I acquired when I was responsible for exchange rate and foreign exchange policies at the Bank of Korea. I believe that the information contained in this book will, to some degree at least, help the general public or employees of financial institutions and firms directly involved with foreign exchange transactions understand the policy side in a broader, more practical manner.

Times were turbulent when I served as Director-General of International Department of the Bank of Korea. The collapse of Lehman Brothers in mid-September 2008 triggered what was to become the biggest global crisis since the Great Depression. We quickly found ourselves facing another foreign currency liquidity crisis after just 10 years.

I worked with 90 staff members of the Bank of Korea and related government officials to develop and implement what turned out to be unprecedented measures. Despite the hardships and difficulties, there were a lot to be proud of, unlike the currency crisis of 1997/8. By reviewing several episodes during this recent tough period, I hope to shed more light on Korea's exchange rate and foreign exchange policies in the coming years.

One of the important measures we implemented was to establish reciprocal currency swap arrangements with the US Federal Reserve, the People's Bank of China, and the Bank of Japan. The swap line with the Federal Reserve was particularly significant. After Lehman Brothers' failure, the Federal Reserve initially provided US dollar funds through currency swaps to only advanced countries, contrary to our expectations. The Bank of Korea, however, successfully established a currency swap arrangement with the Federal Reserve on 30 October 2008, along with Banco Central do Brasil, Banco de Mexico, and Monetary Authority of Singapore, which I believe was based on Korea's heightened profile in the world economy and international financial markets, coupled with its close relationship with the Federal Reserve. It was the first time (and only time so far) that the Fed had set up such swap lines with emerging market economies. Another significant event that followed was our establishment of a similar swap line with the People's Bank of China on December 12 of the same year, which was the first among emerging market economies.

On the day when the Bank of Korea and the Federal Reserve jointly announced the establishment of the currency swap arrangement, the financial markets posted an extraordinary rebound, exceeding expectations. The KOSPI jumped 115.75 points in one day from 968.97 to 1,084.72, while the Korean won strengthened sharply against the US dollar from ₩1,427 to ₩1,250.

I believe that the establishment of the currency swap arrangements greatly helped to minimize the impact of the foreign currency liquidity crisis on our economy and enhance Korea's status in the international financial markets.

Another important task was to decide when to stop providing additional US dollar funds to financial institutions—which was much more difficult than timing the initial provision of such funds. In order to alleviate the shortage of foreign funds, the Bank of Korea provided US dollar funds to financial institutions by auctioning for the first time ever foreign exchange swaps on 21 October and foreign currency loans on 2 December 2008. The Bank had since held auctions of these two alternatively and regularly every week except at the end and beginning of the year and during the Lunar New Year holidays. Thanks to these measures, the foreign currency funding conditions of local commercial banks turned much more favorable from February 2009.

Nevertheless, the exchange rate continued to fluctuate wildly in early March due to negative reports by some members of the foreign press on Korea's foreign currency liquidity and foreign exchange reserves. Yet, despite these circumstances, the Bank of Korea announced a bold move on March 10 to stop providing additional US dollar funds to financial institutions. The significance of this announcement was that we were officially displaying confidence in our ability to overcome the foreign currency liquidity crisis at home and abroad. This became a major turning point in regaining the stability of the local foreign exchange market, as the international financial markets welcomed the move. As a result, the won-dollar exchange rate dropped to ₩1,511.50 on March 10 from ₩1,549.00 on the previous day and further to ₩1,383.50 by the end of that March.

The third experience that I would like to share was the introduction of foreign exchange forward position limits in July 2010, which emerged from six-month-long deliberations between the Ministry of Strategy & Finance and the Bank of Korea. This measure had a major impact on both local commercial banks and the branches of foreign banks, unlike existing regulations on foreign exchange liquidity which applied to Korean banks alone. Some foreign banks argued that the introduction of the foreign exchange forward position ceilings would lead to side effects, such as the widening of imbalances in the swap market, the non-fulfillment of domestic firms' hedging demand, and increases in hedging costs. All this even raised concerns that some foreign banks might close their branches in Korea. Such side effects, however, have not been realized so far, and this system seems to have settled down quite smoothly.

There were also other important measures, such as restrictions on the use of foreign currency loans in August 2007 and July 2010, the Bank of Korea's direct participation in the swap market in September 2007, its auction of foreign exchange swaps in September 2008, and the introduction of a macro-prudential stability levy by the Ministry of Strategy and Finance from 2012. These are all described in the main body of this book.

This book consists of ten chapters, differing markedly from other books in this field from two aspects. First, it comprehensively covers not only exchange rate policy but other policies related to foreign exchange transactions. Secondly, it raises key discussion points in seven of the ten chapters, which are elaborated in some detail so that they can be easily understood. The purpose of the material prior to the key discussion points in each chapter is to provide the requisite knowledge needed for an understanding of the following discussion points. So readers who have already had sufficient exposure to Korea's exchange rate and foreign exchange policies may safely skip those parts and jump right to the key discussion points in each chapter and to the policy tasks ahead in chapter 10.

I sincerely hope that this book will aid policy makers, employees of financial institutions and firms, and others interested in learning more about Korea's exchange rate and foreign exchange policies. The greatest reward for me from having written this book will be if I can contribute to some degree to helping all economic actors prepare themselves against future financial crises. The recent global financial turmoil brought about by the sovereign debt crisis in the Euro zone, for example, brings in its train a high degree of uncertainty, as no one can say for sure where or when it will end.

I am most grateful to all those young and enthusiastic staff members of the Bank of Korea who helped me collect data, and confirm facts in related articles and papers for the publication of this book. I would also like to express my sincere gratitude to Won S. Kim at KB Investment & Securities Research and John R. Balson for helpful comments on the English manuscript. Finally, it would be remiss of me not to thank my wife and our son and daughter, Sekey and Minchung, for their continued encouragement and support.

June 2013

Byungchan Ahn

Chapter 1

Foreign
Exchange
Policy
Framework

Unlike advanced countries, Korea conducts its foreign exchange policy in separation from monetary policy and other macroeconomic policies. Its objectives are to facilitate foreign transactions, maintain equilibrium in the balance of payments, and bring about the stability of the currency's external value.

All authority regarding the establishment and execution of foreign exchange policy, and related supervision and inspection is delegated to the Minister of Strategy and Finance under Korea's Foreign Exchange Transactions Act. The Minister, however, entrusts part of his/her authority to the Governor of the Bank of Korea, the Financial Services Commission, the Governor of the Financial Supervisory Service, and the Commissioner of the Korea Customs Service.

This chapter first outlines the objectives and scope of Korea's foreign exchange policy, and then details the contents of foreign exchange policy, and related supervision and inspection businesses for which each agency is responsible. The types of financial institution subject to foreign exchange policy and the scope of foreign exchange business of each class of financial institution are also described.

1. Objectives and Scope of Foreign Exchange Policy

Emerging Economies Typically Differentiate Foreign Exchange Policy from Monetary Policy

In advanced economies, it is meaningless to distinguish foreign exchange policy from monetary policy.[1] This is because advanced economies including the United States, the eurozone, the United Kingdom and Japan allow completely liberalized transactions of foreign exchange and free-floating exchange rates.[2] In addition, their own currencies are international currencies that are widely used in the global financial marketplace. In other words, the currencies of advanced economies are used when financial institutions, firms or individuals around the world make capital transactions or conduct international trade. Their currencies can also be exchanged against most other currencies without any restrictions in local or foreign markets whenever necessary.

1   Monetary policy refers to the adjustment in monetary aggregates or market interest rates by using instruments, such as policy interest rate, reserve requirements and open market operations, with an ultimate objective to achieve domestic stability of currency value, i.e., price stability. The central bank of each country is responsible for monetary policy.

2   In an exceptional situation, major advanced countries may undertake an intervention in foreign exchange markets on a temporary or short term for maintaining exchange rate stability, but it happens to be rare. For example, the Japan's Ministry of Finance formally intervened in foreign exchange markets for the first time since March 2004 in September 2010, in order to stem a surge in the yen.

Therefore it is generally said that the relationship between local currency denominated finance and foreign currency denominated finance is the same as the relationship of two sides of a coin.

In contrast, emerging market economies need to induce or raise foreign capital for economic development due to a shortage of domestic capital. To this end, their governments deregulate or liberalize foreign exchange and capital transactions. However, history has shown that when financial and economic conditions deteriorate, emerging economies often face a currency crisis or a shortfall in foreign currency liquidity on sudden outflows of foreign capital. For this reason, emerging economies require controls on foreign exchange, and thus the establishment and conduct of foreign exchange policies are important. Considering this, controls on foreign exchange and capital transactions in emerging economies are gradually deregulated, in keeping with the stage of economic development and the degree of development of each country's financial and foreign exchange markets. In addition, the use of their local currencies is liberalized step by step, and limitations on daily exchange rate movements are freed progressively.

Objectives and Scope of Korea's Foreign Exchange Policy

Korea conducts its foreign exchange[3] policy in separation

---

3   The term "foreign exchange" refers to foreign means of payment, foreign

from monetary, fiscal, and other macroeconomic policies. The objectives are to facilitate foreign transactions, maintain equilibrium in the balance of payments, and work for the stability of the currency's external value.[4] To efficiently accomplish these objectives, the Korean government has set basic guidelines for foreign exchange and other external transactions.

Foreign exchange policy is largely divided into exchange rate policy and policy concerning the foreign exchange system. Exchange rate policy determines the exchange rate regime and conducts policy for stable exchange rate management. In Korea, the exchange rate system moved towards allowing gradual enlargement of the daily fluctuation band, in line with economic development and the degree of financial and foreign exchange market development. Korea operated a de facto fixed exchange rate system until the 1970s, and then adopted a multi-currency basket system beginning in February 1980. From March 1990, a shift was made to a market average exchange rate system. On the outbreak of a currency crisis in December 1997, the government transformed its exchange rate regime to a free-floating system, abolishing limits on daily fluctuation. Since then, the Ministry of Strategy and Finance has been conducting exchange rate policy in consultation with the Bank of Korea to

---

currency securities, foreign currency derivatives and foreign currency claims, according to Article of 3 (1) 13 of the Foreign Exchange Transactions Act. The term "foreign currency" means any currency other than domestic currency, according to Article 3 (1) 2 of the Act, and thus "foreign currency" is classed as one of the "foreign means of payment."

4 See Article 1 (Purpose) of the Foreign Exchange Transactions Act.

ensure the stable management of exchange rate.

Meanwhile, policy on the foreign exchange system refers to all policies related to both current transactions and capital transactions of all economic agents including financial institutions, firms and individuals. Any changes in the foreign exchange system may affect exchange rates directly or indirectly through fluctuations of supply and demand for foreign exchange. On the other hand, if sustained exchange rate volatility poses a threat to broader economic activities and financial markets, the government may be required to adjust the foreign exchange system. This shows that exchange rate policy and policy on the foreign exchange system are intricately intertwined. For example, the system of FX forward position limits applicable to both domestic banks and branches of foreign banks has the effect of curbing increases in short-term debt, thereby easing volatility and one-way movements of the exchange rate.

Korea made significant changes to its policy on the foreign exchange system following the currency crisis of December 1997. In 1998, the government virtually liberalized all foreign direct and indirect investments by abolishing ceilings on bond and equity investments by foreigners and shifting foreigners' direct investments from a certification system to a reporting system. In April 1999, the government adopted a full-scale reform of the legal framework applied to foreign exchange and capital transactions, shifting from a system of regulating and managing all transactions to one that ensures the liberalization of transactions and revitalization of market functions. Since then, measures to liberalize foreign exchange and capital transactions have emerged in accordance with expanded overseas investments by domestic firms, financial institutions and individuals. As such, foreign exchange and capital transactions in Korea are deregulated, placing the country's capital liberalization nearly on a par with that of advanced economies.[5]

This book covers Korea's exchange rate policy, foreign exchange reserve management, foreign currency liquidity management, external debt management, capital liberalization and prudential regulation of foreign exchange. Foreign exchange reserve management and foreign currency liquidity management are directly or indirectly related to the exchange rate policy. Capital liberalization and prudential regulation of foreign exchange fall under the policy on the foreign exchange system, while external debt management is intertwined with both of these two policies.

5　With the abolition of the capital transaction permission system from January 2006, almost all of the legal regulations on foreign exchange and capital transactions were removed, as in major advanced countries. However, the actual degree of Korea's liberalization may still fall somewhat short of that of major advanced economies. This is because some procedural regulations, such as ex-ante reporting on capital transactions, reporting on methods of payment and receipt, use of a designated foreign exchange bank for transactions, and submitting supporting documents for transactions, still remain.

2. Policy Authorities and Supervisory Agencies on Foreign Exchange

Foreign Exchange Policy Is Conducted through Foreign Exchange Transaction Laws

Full authority to establish and execute foreign exchange policy lies with the Minister of Strategy and Finance under Korea's Foreign Exchange Transactions Act.[6] The Minister of Strategy and Finance, however, entrusts part of his/her authority on foreign exchange regulation to the Governor of the Bank of Korea and the Financial Services Commission. The Bank of Korea exercises advisory functions concerning the government's exchange rate policy, and takes charge of daily management in foreign exchange markets, including market intervention for the operation of the government's exchange rate policy. Basic guidelines on foreign exchange policy are prescribed by the Foreign Exchange Transactions Act, and its detailed contents are stipulated in the Enforcement Decree of the Foreign Exchange Transactions Act, the Foreign Exchange Transaction Regulation, and foreign-exchange related regulations of the

---

6   In Korea, the legal hierarchy from top to bottom is based on the following: Act, Presidential Decree or Enforcement Decree, and Ordinance of the Executive Ministry, Enforcement Rule or Regulation. The Act is established by the National Assembly, and the Presidential Decree or Enforcement Decree is formulated via the deliberation by the Cabinet, while the Ordinance of the Executive Ministry, Enforcement Rule or Regulation is established by Ministries.

Bank of Korea, the Financial Services Commission, and other agencies.

Meanwhile, in accordance with the Foreign Exchange Transactions Act, the Minister of Strategy and Finance takes overall charge of supervising and inspecting the related businesses[7] of all institutions to which foreign exchange policy applies. The actual work of supervision and inspection, however, is entrusted to the Financial Services Commission and the Governor of the Financial Supervisory Service, while certain joint inspection and inspection business are entrusted to the Governor of the Bank of Korea and the Commissioner of the Korea Customs Service.

Details of each agency's role with regard to foreign exchange policy, including supervision and inspection business, are as follows.

Ministry of Strategy and Finance

All authority regarding the establishment and execution of foreign exchange policy, and related supervision and inspection are vested in the Minister of Strategy and Finance, under Article 23 of the Government Organization Act and the Foreign Exchange Transactions Act. "The Minister of Strategy and Finance shall strive to facilitate foreign exchange transactions

---

7   This book briefly sets out the basic framework for supervising and inspecting the related businesses of all institutions to which foreign exchange policy applies, but does not stipulate regulations in detail.

and other external transactions by imposing restrictions as referred to in this Act only within the minimum extent necessary. The Minister of Strategy and Finance shall endeavor to create a foundation for stable supply and demand of foreign exchange and stabilize the foreign exchange market." Under the Foreign Exchange Transactions Act, the Minister has the following mandate:

- To determine the basic exchange rate for foreign exchange transactions, the rates of buying and selling of foreign exchange, and arbitrated exchange rates, when necessary to ensure harmonious and orderly foreign exchange transactions
- To create, operate and manage the Foreign Exchange Equalization Fund
- Temporary suspension of payment, receipt, or the whole or part of transactions to which this Act applies, or imposition of obligations to safe-keep, deposit or sell means of payment in or to the Bank of Korea, the Foreign Exchange Equalization Fund, or financial institutions in cases of natural calamities, war, or grave and sudden change in domestic and foreign economic conditions
- Imposition of obligations to obtain permission or to deposit part of means of payments acquired in such transactions at the Bank of Korea, the Foreign Exchange Equalization Fund, or financial institutions for any person who intends to perform capital transactions in cases where the balance of payments are liable to be confronted with serious difficulty, or where the movement of capital between Korea and foreign countries is liable to create serious obstacles in carrying out monetary policy, exchange rate policy or other macroeconomic policies

- To require residents holding claims against nonresidents to collect such claims and to repatriate them to Korea
- Registration or authorization and its revocation of foreign exchange agencies, money exchangers, and foreign exchange brokerage companies, and the imposition of penalty surcharges on them
- Supervision of business and prudential regulation on foreign exchange agencies[8]
- To prescribe matters necessary for the payment or receipt to which this Act applies, such as procedures for money exchange, remittance and withdrawal of property
- Reporting on methods of payment or receipt, reporting on export or import of means of payment, and reporting on capital transactions
- To inspect business of foreign exchange agencies and the parties or other persons concerned in connection with transactions to which this Act applies
- Warnings, suspension of transactions, and imposition of fines for negligence on an institution or a person that violates foreign exchange transaction laws

Meanwhile, the Minister of Strategy and Finance may, pursuant to Article 37 of the Enforcement Decree of the Foreign Exchange Transactions Act, delegate or entrust part of his/her authority under Article 23 of the Foreign Exchange Transactions Act to the Governor of the Bank of Korea, the Financial Services Commission, the Governor of the Financial Supervisory Service, the Commissioner of the Korea Customs

---

8 See page 40 for the definition of foreign exchange agencies.

Service, the heads of foreign exchange agencies, or other persons. In addition, under Article 20 (6) of the said Act, the Minister may, pursuant to Article 35 (3) of the Enforcement Decree, entrust his/her power to inspect related businesses of foreign exchange agencies to the Governor of the Bank of Korea, the Governor of the Financial Supervisory Service, the Commissioner of the Korea Customs Service, or other persons.

Bank of Korea

The Bank of Korea (BOK) conducts the following foreign exchange business under Article 82 of the Bank of Korea Act and Article 2–25 of the Foreign Exchange Transaction Regulation.

- Buying and selling of foreign exchange, and transactions of derivatives
- Holding and operating foreign currency funds and foreign exchange
- Receipt of foreign currency deposits from the Government and their agencies, and domestic financial institutions
- Receipt of deposits from overseas financial institutions, international financial organizations, foreign governments and their agencies, or United Nations' organizations
- Borrowings of foreign currency funds from overseas financial institutions and foreign governments
- Acceptance and guarantee of liabilities
- Investments in and loans to international financial organizations
- Loans of foreign currency funds to foreign exchange banks

Table 1.1 Authority and Inspection Entrusted to the Governor of BOK

Type	Contents of entrusted businesses
Entrusted authority	• Prudential regulation of foreign exchange, such as setting of the minimum reserves for specific foreign currency liabilities,[1] setting and management of standards for calculation on FX position limit of foreign exchange banks, and regulation on the method of raising and operating foreign currency funds • Receipt of report on the registration, changes in registered matters, and closure of money exchange business • Supervision of, and orders necessary for the supervision of, money exchangers (excluding money exchangers in open ports) and foreign exchange brokers. Cancellation of registration of money exchangers, and restrictions on or suspension of business of money exchangers (excluding money exchangers in open ports) and foreign exchange brokers • Conduction of business relevant to operation and management of the Foreign Exchange Equalization Fund • In cases where the permission on payment or receipt should be obtained from the Minister of Strategy and Finance, authority to grant permission on such payment or receipt • Receipt of report on methods of payment or receipt for transactions set by the Minister • Receipt of report on capital transactions • Request for report to foreign exchange agencies in cases for managing business entrusted and necessary for preparing statistics related to foreign exchange • Exemption from duty to collect claims, and granting of permission on the extension of such collection period • Administrative dispositions against any person to whom the inspection of the Bank of Korea applies
Entrusted inspection business	• Inspection of money exchangers (excluding money exchangers in open ports), foreign exchange brokers and the trading partners and persons concerned, persons subject to the report relevant to the business performed by the Governor of the Bank of Korea entrusted by the Minister, and financial institutions referred to in Article 11 of the Bank of Korea Act among foreign exchange agencies to which the prudential regulation of the Governor of the Bank of Korea applies.[2]

1. The Monetary Policy Committee of the Bank of Korea, recognizing the setting of the minimum ratio as intrinsically within its authority, decides the minimum ratio of reserves which each banking institution must maintain.
2. The inspection of financial institutions must be conducted by the method that the Governor of the Bank of Korea demands from the Governor of the Financial Supervisory Service, or participates jointly in the inspection conducted by him.

- Sale and purchase of precious metals
- Receipt of local currency deposits from foreign central banks
- Conclusion of correspondent agreements

In addition, under Article 83 of the Bank of Korea Act, the Bank of Korea exercises an advisory function over the government's policies on exchange rates, foreign currency loans and deposits of banking institutions, and the setting of foreign exchange overbought and oversold position limits on them. The Governor of the Bank of Korea also exercises the authority and inspection business entrusted by the Minister of Strategy and Finance, pursuant to Articles 23 and 20 (6) of the Foreign Exchange Transactions Act and Articles 37 (3) and 35 of its Enforcement Decree. Besides this, the Bank of Korea takes charge of the business of the foreign exchange information concentration agency that relays, concentrates and interchanges data on foreign exchange transactions, payments or receipts under Article 25 (2) of the Foreign Exchange Transactions Act and Article 10-14 (1) of the Foreign Exchange Transaction Regulation. Details are described in Table 1.1.

Financial Services Commission and Financial Supervisory Service

The Financial Services Commission (FSC) exercises the authority entrusted by the Minister of Strategy and Finance, pursuant to Article 23 of the Foreign Exchange Transactions

Table 1.2 Authority and Inspection Entrusted to FSC and FSS

	Type	Contents of entrusted businesses
Financial Services Commission	Entrusted authority	• Supervision of, and orders necessary for the supervision of, foreign exchange agencies • Warning, restriction on or suspension of foreign exchange agency's business • Request for report to foreign exchange agencies to ensure the effectiveness of the Act • Prudential regulation of foreign exchange, such as management of FX position limit of foreign exchange agencies excluding foreign exchange banks, regulation on ratio of assets and liabilities in foreign currency • Administrative dispositions against any person subject to the inspection of the Governor of FSS, setting of standards for accounting of offshore business accounts and foreign exchange agencies' FX accounts, and setting of risk management standards incidental to FX business
Governor of FSS	Entrusted authority	• Receipt of report on the establishment, closure or modification of foreign exchange agencies' domestic business office
	Entrusted inspection	• Inspection of foreign exchange agencies, and their trading counterparts and persons concerned

Act and Article 37 (2) of its Enforcement Decree.[9] The Governor of the Financial Supervisory Service exercises the authority and inspection business entrusted by the Minister of

9 The Financial Services Commission may further delegate part of the authority entrusted from the Minister of Strategy and Finance to the Governor of the Financial Supervisory Service, pursuant to Article 37 (2) of the Enforcement Decree.

Strategy and Finance, pursuant to Articles 23 and 20 (6) of the Act and Articles 37 (4) and 35 (3) 2 of its Enforcement Decree. Details are described in Table 1.2.

Foreign Exchange Agency

The heads of foreign exchange agencies conduct businesses entrusted by the Minister of Strategy and Finance, pursuant to Article 23 of the Foreign Exchange Transactions Act and Article 37 (5) of its Enforcement Decree. Details are as follows:

- Reporting on the method of such payment or receipt in cases where he/she makes any settlement by extinguishing or offsetting a claim and liability with the method such as a setoff pursuant to subparagraph 1 of Article 16 of the Act (limited to matters publicly announced by the Minister of Strategy and Finance)
- Reporting on capital transactions pursuant to Article 18 (1) and (3) of the Act (limited to matters publicly announced by the Minister of Strategy and Finance)
- Warning pursuant to Article 19 of the Act or suspension of, or restrictions on, related foreign exchange transactions or payment (limited where credit card companies under the Specialized Credit Finance Business Act do so to cardholder members)
- Request for report pursuant to Article 20 (2) of the Act (limited to cases for managing the business entrusted under this paragraph)

The present Foreign Exchange Transactions Act strives to secure efficiency in foreign exchange transactions through such ways that they are mostly made through foreign exchange banks, and that part of the administrative authority such as confirmation, receipt of reporting and ex-post management of foreign exchange transactions is also entrusted to the heads of foreign exchange banks.

Other Agencies

Other agencies related to foreign exchange transactions include the Korea Customs Service, the National Tax Service, the Financial Intelligence Unit, the foreign exchange information concentration agency, and the foreign exchange information analysis agency.

The Minister of Strategy and Finance, pursuant to Articles 23 and 20 (6) of the Foreign Exchange Transactions Act and Articles 37 (1) and 35 (3) 3 of its Enforcement Decree, delegates part of his/her authority and inspection business to the Korea Customs Service. In accordance with the delegation, the Commissioner of the Korea Customs Service takes charge of receipts of reports on exporting and importing by carrying means of payment (referring to the means of foreign payment, local currency, and traveler's checks and bank checks denoted in the local currency) exceeding 10,000 US dollars, receipts of reports on export/import of means of payment or securities, supervision of money exchangers in open ports, and inspection activities and penalty imposition on parties and persons concerned in export and import transactions as well as services transactions and capital transactions directly related thereto.

In this regard, the heads of foreign exchange agencies shall notify the Commissioner of Korea Customs Service of such transactions as buying or selling foreign exchange exceeding 10,000 US dollars by a person on the same day, payment or receipt of export/import transaction amount, payment or receipt of service transaction amount, and payment of overseas emigration expense exceeding 10,000 US dollars by the 10th day of the following month on a monthly basis.

The Minister of Strategy and Finance strengthened the reporting system of foreign exchange transaction information to the Korea Customs Service in order to prevent the illegal flight of foreign exchange and an evasion of taxes on offshore income which may occur due to the liberalization of foreign exchange transactions. The heads of foreign exchange agencies shall notify the Commissioner of the National Tax Service of transactions such as purchase and sale or payment of foreign exchange exceeding 10,000 US dollars per case, payment of overseas travel expenses to any overseas student or any overseas sojourner exceeding 100,000 US dollars per person annually. In June 2008, the ceiling on purchase amount of foreign real estate for the purpose of investment was abolished. In accordance with this, the Governor of the Bank of Korea and the head of a designated correspondent bank who receive the report of purchase of overseas real estate for ex-post facto monitoring shall notify the Commissioner of the National Tax Service of the contents of such transactions.

The Korea Financial Intelligence Unit was founded on November 2001 under the Act on Reporting and Use of Certain Financial Transaction Information. The purpose of its establishment was to prevent any money laundering activities of criminal funds utilizing financial institutions and illegal flight of foreign exchange, in the aftermath of the September 11 attack on the United States. In accordance with this Act, financial institutions shall report suspicious transactions exceeding 10 million won for financial transaction denominated in Korean currency, and those exceeding 5,000 dollars for financial transaction denominated in US dollar to the Korea Financial Intelligence Unit. In addition, the Minister of Strategy and Finance designated international terror groups as the object of financial sanctions according to the Foreign Exchange Transactions Act and Guidelines of Payments and Receipts for Implementation of Duties for International Peace and Maintenance of Security. Residents shall get permission from the Governor of the Bank of Korea so as to complete payment and receipt with such an entity under financial sanction.

Meanwhile, the Minister of Strategy and Finance, pursuant to Article 25 (2) of the Foreign Exchange Transactions Act and Article 10-14 (1) of the Foreign Exchange Transaction Regulation, designated the Bank of Korea as the foreign exchange information concentration agency to relay, concentrate and interchange data on foreign exchange transactions, payments or receipts. The Minister also designated the International Finance Center as the foreign exchange information analysis agency to analyze such data. Foreign exchange agencies shall notify, when conducting businesses such as foreign exchange transactions or payments, the foreign exchange information concentration agency of its contents. The foreign exchange information concentration agency may furnish the data on foreign exchange transactions stipulated by the Minister's regulation under Article 10−14 (4) of the Foreign Exchange Transaction Regulation to the foreign exchange information analysis agency.

3. Financial Institutions Subject to Foreign Exchange Policy

Under foreign exchange transaction laws, foreign exchange policies are applied to a foreign exchange agency, a foreign exchange brokerage company and a money exchanger. According to Article 10 of the Foreign Exchange Transactions Act, "foreign exchange agencies" is used as a general term to include these three types of institutions.

Foreign Exchange Agency

The term "foreign exchange agency" is defined as financial institution which is registered with the Minister of Strategy and Finance in advance to operate foreign exchange businesses under Article 8 (1) of the Act. According to Article 3 (1) 17 of the Act, eligible foreign exchange agencies consist of financial institutions referred to in Article 38 (excluding subparagraphs 14 and 15) of the "Act on the Establishment, etc. of Financial Services Commission," the Korea Development Bank, the Korea Finance Corporation, the Export-Import Bank of Korea, the Industrial Bank of Korea, and the Post Office.

Of these, financial institutions referred to in Article 38 (excluding subparagraphs 14 and 15) of the "Act on the Establishment, etc. of Financial Services Commission" are as follows:

- Banks established with authorization under the Banking Act
- Financial investment business entities, securities finance companies, merchant banks, and companies performing affairs of transfer agency under the Capital Market and Financial Investment Business Act
- Insurers under the Insurance Business Act
- Mutual savings banks and their National Federation under the Mutual Savings Banks Act
- Credit unions and their National Federation under the Credit Unions Act
- Specialized credit financial business companies and dealers engaged concurrently in credit business under the Specialized Credit Financial Business Act
- Credit business sector of the National Agricultural Cooperative Federation under the Agricultural Cooperatives Act
- Credit business sector of the National Federation of Fisheries Cooperatives under the Fisheries Cooperatives Act

Scope of Foreign Exchange Business by Financial Institution

Foreign exchange banks among foreign exchange agencies can deal with all foreign exchange businesses prescribed in Article

8 (2) of the Foreign Exchange Transactions Act and Article 14 of its Enforcement Decree. Foreign exchange banks refer to financial institutions under the Banking Act, banking sector of the National Agricultural Cooperative Federation, banking sector of the National Fisheries Cooperative Federation, the Korea Development Bank, the Korea Finance Corporation, the Export-Import Bank of Korea and the Industrial Bank of Korea. Other foreign exchange agencies can conduct such business in so far as it is directly related to the business of the financial institution as prescribed by the Minister of Strategy and Finance. Coverage of foreign exchange business by financial institution is described in Table 1.3. Any institution may, however, engage only in money exchange business, even if it is not a financial institution.

Under Article 3 (1) 16 of the Act and Article 6 of its Enforcement Decree, foreign exchange business refers to one of following businesses.

- Issuance or purchase/sale of foreign exchange
- Payment, collection and receipt between Korea and a foreign country
- Deposits, lending and borrowing of money, or guarantee denominated or paid in foreign currency with residents
- Deposits, lending and borrowing of money, or guarantee with nonresidents[10]

10 According to Article 3 (1) of the Foreign Exchange Transactions Act, the term "resident" means any private person domiciled or resident in Korea, and any company whose main office is located in Korea, while the term "nonresident" means any private person and any company based outside of Korea. But the branch offices, local offices or other offices of nonresidents located in Korea shall be deemed residents.

Table 1.3 Scope of Foreign Exchange Business by Financial Institution

	Scope of foreign exchange business
Foreign exchange bank	All foreign exchange businesses listed in Article 3 (1) 16 of the Foreign Exchange Transactions Act and Article 6 of its Enforcement Decree
Merchant bank	Businesses excluding the following businesses among foreign exchange banks' FX business • Deposits (excluding deposits which can be denominated or paid in foreign currency by foreign exchange agencies and financial institutions abroad) • Issuance of a letter of credit and payment between Korea and foreign countries that are not directly related to the businesses stipulated in the Capital Market and Financial Investment Business Act
Post Office	Foreign exchange business listed below • Buying of money orders demonstrated in foreign currency (including payment orders by mail or wire) • Buying and selling of foreign currencies and traveler's checks (in cases of nonresidents or foreigners recognized as residents, selling of foreign currencies and traveler's checks is limited within the sold amount in exchange for the means of domestic payment) • Issuance and selling of money orders denominated in foreign currency to any person who is going to make payments stipulated in the Foreign Exchange Transaction Regulation
Others	Business directly related to the financial institutions' business among the following businesses as determined and publicly announced by the Minister of Strategy and Finance • Buying and selling of foreign currency bonds • Issue, and buying and selling of foreign currency securities • Buying and selling of securities and bonds denominated or paid in domestic currency with nonresidents • Borrowing and lending or guarantee of deposits and cash which can be denominated or paid in foreign currency with residents • Borrowing and lending or guarantee of deposits and cash with nonresidents

- Buying and selling of foreign means of payment
- Derivatives transaction
- Insurance transaction denominated in foreign currency with residents, or insurance transaction with nonresidents
- Facilities loan denominated in foreign currency
- Business operated separately by investor under his/her entrustment on judgment of investment
- Trust business

- Sales and purchase of securities or bonds denominated or paid in domestic currency with nonresidents
- Trust, insurance and transactions of derivatives (limited to those related to foreign exchange) between residents, or trust, insurance and transactions of derivatives between residents and nonresidents
- Facility loans denominated in foreign currency (referring to facility loans under the Specialized Credit Financial Business Act)
- Other business incidental to the business listed above

Foreign Exchange Brokerage Company

A foreign exchange brokerage company refers to any institution which intends to engage in the following business (hereinafter referred to as the "foreign exchange brokerage"); a brokerage of purchase, sale, exchange and lending of foreign currencies; brokerage of derivative transactions based on foreign currencies; other businesses related to the business above. Any institution which intends to engage in a foreign exchange brokerage shall prepare capital, facilities and professional human resources as prescribed by the Enforcement Decree of the Foreign Exchange Transactions Act, and then shall obtain authorization from the Minister of Strategy and Finance under Article 9 of the Act. Accordingly, the Minister takes charge of the supervision and inspection of foreign exchange brokerage companies under Articles 11 and 20 of the Act. Actually, the Minister's authority for restrictions on or suspension of the operations of foreign exchange brokerage companies, and inspection business on them are entrusted to the Governor of the Bank of Korea under Articles 35 (3) 1 and 37 (3) of the Enforcement Decree of the Act. As of now, there are ten foreign exchange brokerage companies[11] in Korea.

Money Exchanger

A money exchanger refers to any person who registers with the Ministry of Strategy and Finance in advance in order to engage in only the money exchange business under Article 8 (3) of the Foreign Exchange Transactions Act. Actually, the Minister's authority over the supervision of money exchangers including

---

11 Korea Money Brokerage Corp., Seoul Money Brokerage Services, Ltd., KIDB Money Brokerage Corp., Integrated Platform Services Corporation, ICAP Foreign Exchange Brokerage (Korea) limited, Tullet Prebon Money Brokerage (Korea) Limited, GFI, Nittan Capital Money Brokerage (Korea) Limited, GFI Korea Money Brokerage Limited, Tradition Korea Limited, and BGC Capital Markets and Foreign Exchange Broker (Korea) LTD.

Figure 1.1. Foreign Exchange Policy Framework

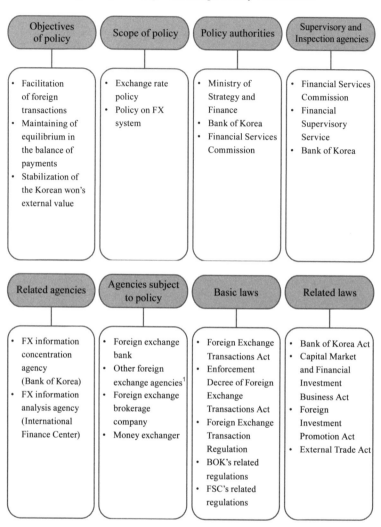

1. financial investment business entities, securities finance companies, merchant banks, post offices, insurers, mutual savings banks, credit unions, specialized credit financial business companies, credit card companies

the registration is entrusted to the Governor of the Bank of Korea under Article 37 (3) of the Enforcement Decree of the Act. Money exchange business includes a purchase and sale of foreign currency, and a purchase of a traveler's check issued in a foreign country. In principle, a money exchanger cannot deal in sales of foreign currency, but can only engage in purchases of it. But money exchangers may reexchange to any nonresident in cases where he/she intends to reexchange within the sold record of the means of foreign payment to foreign exchange agencies or money exchangers in exchange for the means of domestic payment during his sojourning period since his recent entry date to Korea, in cases where he/she intends to reexchange the amount acquired in the casino of such a money exchanger, and in the case of unused money. There were 1,205 registered money exchangers as of the end of 2012.

Chapter 2

Exchange
Rate
Policy

In Korea, the ultimate authority and responsibility for exchange rate policy and the stability of the foreign exchange market are given to the Minister of Strategy and Finance under the Foreign Exchange Transactions Act. The actual decision making process of exchange rate policy, however, is made based on close consultation between the Ministry of Strategy and Finance and the Bank of Korea. The Bank of Korea takes charge of daily management of the foreign exchange market, including market intervention.

This chapter first describes how exchange rate policy has been conducted in Korea, and then briefly explains the impact of exchange rates on the economy. Finally, three main issues—an assessment of the present level of the exchange rate, exchange rate volatility, and the relationship between the interest rate and the exchange rate—are discussed.

1. Exchange Rate Policy

Legal Authority on Exchange Rate Policy

In Korea, the ultimate authority and responsibility for exchange rate policy and the stability of the foreign exchange market are given to the Minister of Strategy and Finance under the Foreign Exchange Transactions Act. Article 4 (2) of the Act prescribes that "the Minister of Strategy and Finance shall endeavor to create a foundation for balanced supply and demand of foreign exchange and a stable foreign exchange market, and shall devise policies thereof." Article 5 (1) of the Act stipulates that "the Minister of Strategy and Finance may determine the basic exchange rate for foreign exchange transactions, rate of purchase and sale of foreign exchange, and arbitrated exchange rate, if it is necessary to do so for harmonious and orderly foreign exchange transactions."

Legally, there are no grounds on which the Bank of Korea has authority or responsibility for exchange rate policy or the stabilization of the foreign exchange market. Article 83 of the Bank of Korea Act states that "the Bank of Korea shall exercise an advisory function over the government's policies on exchange rates, foreign currency loans and deposits of foreign exchange banks, and the setting of foreign exchange overbought and oversold position ceilings on them." This is interpreted as a kind of counseling clause without legal compulsory force. The buying and selling of foreign currencies in the foreign exchange market by the Bank of Korea pertain to Article 82 of the

Table 2.1 Main Provisions of Laws on Exchange Rate Policy

Foreign Exchange Transactions Act

Article 4 (Striving for Facilitation of Foreign Transactions)

(2) The Minister of Strategy and Finance shall endeavor to create a foundation for stable
supply and demand of foreign exchange and to stabilize the foreign exchange market, and shall
devise policies thereof.

Article 5 (Exchange Rates)

(1) The Minister of Strategy and Finance may determine the basic exchange rate for foreign
exchange transactions, rate of purchase and sale of foreign exchange, and arbitrated exchange
rate (hereafter referred to as the "basic exchange rate"), if it is necessary to do so for
harmonious and orderly foreign exchange transactions.

Article 13 (Foreign Exchange Equalization Fund)

(1) In order to facilitate foreign exchange transactions, a Foreign Exchange Equalization Fund
shall be established as a fund under Article 5 of the National Finance Act.

Foreign Exchange Transaction Regulation

Article 2–25 (Foreign Exchange Business of the BOK)

The BOK may conduct the following foreign exchange business.

Bank of Korea Act

Article 82 (Foreign Exchange Business, etc)

The Bank of Korea may, subject to the authorization of the Minister of Strategy and
Finance, engage in the following business:

1. Foreign exchange business operations and the holding of foreign exchange;

2. Acceptance of deposits from foreign banking institutions, international financial
organizations, foreign governments and their agencies, or United Nations' organizations; and

3. Buying and selling of precious metals.

Article 83 (Advice on Foreign Exchange Rate Policy, etc)

The Bank of Korea shall exercise an advisory function concerning the Government's policies
on exchange rates, foreign currency loans and deposits of banking institutions, and the setting
of foreign exchange overbought and oversold position limits on them.

Bank of Korea Act and Article 2–25 of the Foreign Exchange Transaction Regulation.

In the meantime, in the event that the Minister of Strategy and Finance demands the Bank of Korea intervene in the foreign exchange market with resources of the Foreign Exchange Equalization Fund, the Bank of Korea has a responsibility to carry out the request. The Minister of Strategy and Finance entrusts his/her authority for dealing with practical matters related to the operation and management of the Foreign Exchange Equalization Fund to the Bank of Korea under foreign exchange transaction laws.[12]

Conduct of Exchange Rate Policy

A country's exchange rate policy comprises choosing an exchange rate system and determining market intervention. In Korea, the exchange rate system has been revised several times, in line with economic development and changing international conditions. At the outbreak of the currency crisis in December 1997, the exchange rate regime was effectively transformed into a free-floating system with the abolition of restrictions on the daily fluctuation band.[13]

12 Article 13 (Foreign Exchange Equalization Fund) and 23 (Delegation and Entrustment of Authority) of the Foreign Exchange Transactions Act, and Article 15 (Delegation and Entrustment of Authority) of its Enforcement Decree.
13 Restrictions on daily fluctuation band following the introduction of Market Average Exchange Rate System in March 1990 were as follows.

Legally, intervention in the foreign exchange market is entrusted to the Minister of Strategy and Finance, who has ultimate authority and responsibility on exchange rate policy. The actual decision making process, however, is made based on close consultation between the Ministry of Strategy and Finance and the Bank of Korea. The Bank of Korea takes charge of daily management of foreign exchange market policy, including market intervention, as in the case in other countries. This is because the Bank of Korea performs the settlement function for the local currency with commercial banks as the central bank, and has the appropriate system with sufficient trained staff to conduct such intervention. Furthermore, the Bank of Korea has established channels to collect information on the foreign exchange market via commercial banks.

Funding Resources for Market Intervention

The government established the Foreign Exchange Equalization Fund to facilitate foreign exchange transactions, and the Minister of Strategy and Finance takes charge of its operation and management. The Minister may intervene in the foreign exchange market by using local and foreign currencies from the Fund in the event it is deemed necessary to stabilize the foreign

1990. 3	1991. 9	1992. 7	1993. 10	1994. 11	1995. 12	1997. 11	1997. 12
+0.4%	+0.6%	+0.8%	+1.0%	+1.5%	+2.25%	+10.0%	abolished

exchange market, and entrusts the conduct of practical affairs related to the operation and management of the Fund to the Bank of Korea.

Financial resources of the Foreign Exchange Equalization Fund were mainly raised by issuing Foreign Exchange Equalization Fund Bonds. The bonds denominated in local currency issued from March 1987 have been replaced by treasury bonds issued with the purpose of stabilizing the foreign exchange market since November 2003. The government has to obtain the consent of the National Assembly on an annual basis, regarding the ceiling on the issuance of treasury bonds for the purpose of stabilizing the foreign exchange market. For this reason, there is a budgetary limitation when raising financial resources for market intervention. The outstanding balance of treasury bonds totaled 128,581.9 billion won as of end-2011.

Table 2.2 Issuance of Treasury Bonds for
the Purpose of Stabilizing the Foreign Exchange Market

(Billions of won)

	2005	2006	2007	2008	2009	2010	2011
Issuance of treasury bonds	21,900.0	20,200.0	19,100.0	15,781.9	26,600.0	35,415.7	16,000.0
Outstanding balance	61,000.0	72,000.0	83,000.0	88,781.9	96,581.9	112,581.9	128,581.9

Sources: Ministry of Strategy and Finance; National Assembly of Korea

It is known that the Bank of Korea has a role in providing a portion of the financial resources for market intervention through consultation with the Ministry of Strategy and Finance in the event it is deemed necessary, considering the developments of foreign exchange market and monetary conditions. If the Bank of Korea buys US dollars in the foreign exchange market, local currency funds equivalent to it are injected into the financial markets. At the same time, the Bank of Korea absorbs the excessive money supply arising in the process of market intervention through the issuance of Monetary Stabilization Bonds, which is known as sterilized intervention. As of the end of 2012, the outstanding balance of Monetary Stabilization Bonds amounted to 163,070 billion won.

Exchange Rate Developments since Currency Crisis of 1997

Since the shift to a free-floating exchange rate system in December 1997, the Korean won has fluctuated against the US dollar, based on changing economic fundamentals, inflows and outflows of foreign securities investment funds, international financial market trends including the US dollar's exchange value, and changing market expectations. In particular, the won showed volatile movements in the wake of the 1997 Asian currency crisis and the 2008 global financial crisis.

In the domestic foreign exchange market, the won/dollar exchange rate,[14] which stood at ₩844.90 at the end of 1996, soared sharply to the record high of ₩1,962.00 on 23 December 1997 in the midst of the currency crisis. The won/dollar rate subsequently continued to drop back rapidly as an excess supply of foreign exchange persisted due to a large current account surplus, increased inflows of foreign equity investment funds, and improved foreign currency liquidity among financial institutions. It dropped to ₩1,104.40 on 4 September 2000.

From late-November 2000, the won/dollar exchange rate returned to its upward trend, reflecting unstable factors such as a slowdown in domestic economic activity, a liquidity crisis and delayed restructuring at the Hyundai Group, and yen weakness due to a financial crisis in Japan. It jumped to ₩1,365.20 on 4 April 2001, and then hovered around ₩1,300 for about a year.

From April 2002 to October 2007, the won/dollar exchange rate continued on a declining trend. It fell sharply to ₩1,165.60 on 22 July 2002, affected by the recovery in domestic economic activity, and sharp weakness of the US dollar owing to a widening current account deficit and the ENRON accounting scandal in the US. From October 2004, the won/dollar rate again exhibited a downward trend, reflecting US dollar weakness, excess supply of foreign exchange, and one-sided expectations of won appreciation. By 29 April 2005, the Korean won closed at ₩997.10 against dollar. From December 2005, the won/dollar rate declined further due to US dollar weakness and a sharp increase in FX forward selling by export firms and

14 A rise in the won/dollar exchange rate means the Korean won's depreciation against the US dollar, whereas a fall in the won/dollar rate means the Korean won's appreciation against the US dollar. In other books or international financial markets, the dollar/won rate or dollar-won rate is often expressed with the same meaning as the won/dollar rate in this book.

asset management companies dealing with foreign securities investments. As a result, it dropped to ₩900.70 at the end of October 2007, a record low since the Asian financial crisis.

From March 2008, however, the Korean won depreciated sharply in the wake of the global financial crisis, triggered by the Lehman Brothers' collapse in mid-September, a rapid outflow of foreign currency funds and deteriorating conditions for domestic banks' foreign currency liquidity. The won/dollar rate soared to ₩1,570.30 on 2 March 2009, the highest level reached in the global financial crisis following Lehman Brothers' collapse, and continued to fluctuate wildly in early March due to negative reports by some foreign press commentators on Korea's foreign currency liquidity and foreign exchange reserves.

Despite these circumstances, the Bank of Korea announced a bold move on 10 March 2009 to stop providing additional US dollar funds to financial institutions. This became a major turning point in regaining the stability of the local foreign exchange market. As a result, the Korean won began to appreciate sharply, and thus the won/dollar rate fell to ₩1,104.10 on 26 April 2010. This reflected the easing of global financial unrest, a large current account surplus led by increased exports, and inflows of foreign securities investment funds. The won/dollar rate temporarily rose to ₩1,253.30 around late-May due to concerns over spreading eurozone contagion, and rising geopolitical risk on the Korean peninsula after the findings of the investigation into the sinking of the 'Cheonan,' a Korean naval frigate, were announced.

From July, however, the won/dollar rate turned to a

declining trend, falling to ₩1,134.80 by the end of December 2010. This reflected the soundness of economic fundamentals, such as high growth and a current account surplus, on the heels of increased inflows of foreign portfolio investment funds and US dollar weakness following the Fed's quantitative easing. The won rate dropped further to ₩1,050 on 27 July 2011, the lowest level in the three years after the Lehman Brothers' collapse. But it rebounded to ₩1,195.80 by 26 September, as a result of the downgrade of the US sovereign credit rating, concerns over the sovereign debt crisis in some eurozone countries, and geopolitical risks in relation to North Korea. Between October 2011 and May 2012, the won/dollar rate fluctuated within a

Figure 2.1 KRW/USD Exchange Rate Movements, 1997–2012

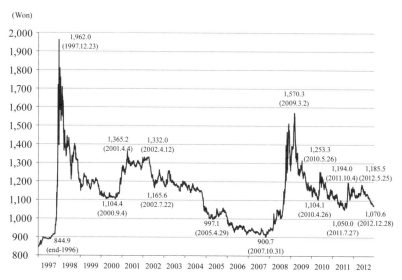

Source: Bank of Korea

range of ₩1,100 and ₩1,185.

From late-May, however, the Korean won marked a sustained appreciating trend against the dollar as expectations of global liquidity inflows to Korea increased, influenced by the inflow of foreigners' stock investment funds, major countries' announcements of additional quantitative easing policies, and the ECB's Outright Monetary Transactions (OMT) program. As of the end of 2012, the Korean won traded at ₩1,070.60 per dollar.

The amount of FX spot trading by domestic foreign exchange banks stood at five billion US dollars on an annual basis from 2000 to 2003, but it began to increase rapidly from 2004. In particular, the volume of FX spot trading increased largely due to a surge in overseas securities investments by individual Koreans, and an increase in domestic bond investments by nonresidents, reaching 19.7 US billion dollars in 2008. The volume, however, sharply decreased to 13.9 billion US dollars in 2009 owing to the global financial crisis. As the local foreign exchange market regained stability, the volume increased to reach 18.0 billion US dollars in 2012, but still short of the level seen in 2008. In 2012, the volume of FX spot trading accounted for 39.6 per cent of total foreign exchange transactions including forwards, FX swaps, currency swaps, and options.

Table 2.3 FX Spot Trading Volume

(Daily average, billions of US dollars, percent)

	2000	2005	2007	2008	2009	2010	2011	2012
Spot Turnover[1]	5.49 (64.9)	9.68 (46.6)	18.52 (45.6)	19.69 (40.5)	13.91 (36.5)	16.58 (39.6)	19.09 (40.8)	17.96 (39.6)
via FX brokers[2]	2.38	4.52	8.25	7.81	5.83	7.66	9.06	9.12
Total FX Turnover[3]	8.46	20.78	40.65	48.67	38.08	41.89	46.83	45.38

1. Figures in ( ) represent the shares of spot turnover in total FX turnover.
2. Based on transactions via FX brokers in the interbank market.
3. Spot, forwards, FX swaps, currency swaps and currency option transactions (including customer and interbank market transactions)
Sources: Bank of Korea, Foreign Exchange Market Trends during 2012, Press Release, 29 January 2013; Developments of Foreign Exchange Transactions of Foreign Exchange Banks during 2012, Press Release (in Korean), 20 February 2013.

2. Changes in the Exchange Rate and Their Impact

Changes in the exchange rate have a large impact on firms and individuals as well as the overall economy, such as exports/imports, the current account, inflation and economic growth. In reality, the impact of exchange rates on the economy occurs through very sophisticated channels. This is because changes in the exchange rate interact with changes in macro variables. For this reason, the influence of the exchange rate on an economy is analyzed by employing macro econometric models, which consist of many simultaneous equations. For example, according to the press report released in 22 January 2010, the Bank of

Korea estimated that should the won/dollar exchange rate fall (i.e., won appreciate) by 10 percent on average, the trade account and current account surpluses would shrink annually by five and seven billion US dollars, respectively. In addition, annual GDP growth would decline by about 0.4 percentage points, while inflation (in terms of consumer prices) would decline by about 0.5 percentage points a year.

Here is the basic mechanism of changes in the exchange rate and their impact on the macro economy. For example, if the won/dollar exchange rate rises (i.e., won depreciates), export volume and value increase because domestic firms can make their dollar-denominated export goods more cheaply than their foreign competitors. But import volume and amount decrease because the won-denominated prices of imported goods are more expensive, pushing down demand for such products. Accordingly, the trade account and the current account improve in Korea's favor. If the prices of imported goods rise due to the increase in the exchange rate, domestic demand, such as consumption and facilities investment of imported goods weaken. But, as the export volume expands, economic growth and employment expand in Korea given its high dependency on exports. However, as the won/dollar exchange rate rises, it brings about an increase in the won-denominated price of imported raw materials. This would exacerbate domestic inflation, and heighten the burden of principal and interest payments for financial institutions with heavy foreign currency liabilities.

Conversely, if the won/dollar exchange rate falls (i.e., won appreciates), the volume and amount of exported goods decrease because domestic firms raise the dollar-denominated prices of export goods to ensure their viability. The prices of Korean goods are also more expensive than those of competing products from different countries. But the volume and amount of imported goods increase because the won-denominated prices of imported goods decline and the demand for imported goods increases. As a result, the trade account and the current account deteriorate. The decline in export volume slows economic growth and exacerbates employment conditions, but the increase in import volume has a positive

Figure 2.2 Basic Transmission Mechanism of Effect of Decrease in KRW/USD Exchange Rate

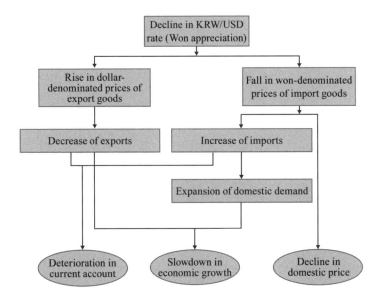

effect on economic growth and employment conditions by expanding domestic demand such as consumption and facilities investment of imported goods. In addition, the decline in the exchange rate brings stability to domestic prices by lowering the price of imported goods and reducing the price of products manufactured by using raw materials imported from foreign countries. Furthermore, it has a positive effect in alleviating the burden of principal and interest payments for financial institutions with heavy foreign currency liabilities.

So far, we have looked into the basic mechanism whereby changes in exchange rate influence the economy, and it assumed that other factors excluding exchange rate did not alter. But in reality, various factors including exchange rates affect the economy. For this reason, despite the negative factors that come with won appreciation, it may bring about greater exports and economic expansion, thanks to favorable global conditions, improved product quality via technological development, and reduced costs as a result of restructuring. For example, in 2010, the won fell by an average of 9.4 percent against the US dollar (that is, the value of the won appreciated) compared with the previous year, but the amount of exports increased by 28.3 percent. In contrast, despite won depreciation, exports might slow as the world struggles with recessionary pressure.

In particular, we have to keep in mind that won depreciation is not even necessarily good for economic growth. If the won/dollar rate rises excessively, it may result in severe side-effects such as accelerated inflation, sluggish domestic demand, economic recession and higher unemployment. On the other hand, even if the exchange rate declines, but still remains higher than appropriate, then it may be good for exports and economic growth.

Therefore, exchange rate policy should be conducted by taking comprehensive account of the positive and negative effects of the exchange rate on each sector of the domestic economy as well as overseas economic and financial conditions. The exchange rate, in principle, should be allowed to float freely according to the supply and demand of foreign exchange, reflecting economic fundamentals, but it is desirable to alleviate sharp fluctuations if possible.

Table 2.4 Exchange Rate and Main Economic Indicators

	2005	2006	2007	2008	2009	2010	2011	2012
KRW/USD (%)[1]	−10.5	−6.7	−2.7	18.7	15.7	−9.4	−4.2	1.7
Current ccount ($bil.)	18.6	14.1	21.8	3.2	32.8	29.4	26.1	43.3
Trade account ($bil.)[2]	23.2	16.1	14.6	−13.3	40.4	41.2	30.8	28.3
Export growth (%)	12.0	14.4	14.1	13.6	−13.9	28.3	19.0	−1.3
Import growth (%)	16.4	18.4	15.3	22.0	−25.8	31.6	23.3	−0.9
GDP growth (%)	4.0	5.2	5.1	2.3	0.3	6.3	3.6	2.0
Inflation rate (%)[3]	2.8	2.2	2.5	4.7	2.8	3.0	4.0	2.2

1. Indicates percentage change from the previous year, based on annual averages of daily closing rates in the Seoul foreign exchange market during the period. Figures with (+) or (−) signs represent rates of depreciation or appreciation of the won against the US dollar, respectively.
2. Differences of exports and imports on a customs-clearance basis. Figures with (+) or (−) signs represent surpluses or deficits, respectively.
3. Based on the consumer price index (CPI).
Sources: Bank of Korea; Korea Customs Service; Statistics Korea

3. Key Discussion Points

There are three key issues with regard to exchange rates: assessment of the current level of the exchange rate, exchange rate volatility, and the relationship between the interest rate and the exchange rate.

Assessment of the Current Level of Exchange Rate

One of issues discussed most actively is related to assessment of the current level of the exchange rate. As discussed earlier, exchange rates significantly impact exports/imports, the current account, economic growth, and firms' profitability because of Korea's export-dependent economy (58.2 percent of GNI in 2012).

When many analysts and economists discuss exchange rates, they commonly refer to the "appropriate exchange rate" or "equilibrium exchange rate." Accordingly, we have to first clarify concepts of the appropriate exchange rate and equilibrium exchange rate. As to what is the level of the appropriate exchange rate, various economic agents, such as policy authorities, exporting firms, importing firms and individual citizens think differently from each other. For example, if the currency is on the weak side, exporting firms enjoy advantages, such as increased exports and improved profitability. But importing firms suffer disadvantages, such as higher import prices and lower profitability.

Therefore, the appropriate exchange rate may be regarded

as a subjective concept. An assessment of the current level of exchange rate has to be made from the viewpoint of the overall economy, without overemphasizing any particular economic agent. For this reason, as a standard for judgment of the current level, the "equilibrium exchange rate" seems more suited than the "appropriate exchange rate." An equilibrium exchange rate is defined as a rate that simultaneously attains both internal and external equilibria. Internal equilibrium or balance is normally defined as attaining the potential growth rate amid price stability, while external equilibrium or balance is strictly defined as the attainment of an almost evenly-balanced current account position. But, in general, as in the external-balance approach to the determination of long-term equilibrium exchange rate, external balance is defined as being the attainment of some targeted level for the current account balance[15] that is feasible or sustainable over the long run, even though the current account may record a deficit or a surplus.[16] Thus, the equilibrium exchange rate may be defined as the level at which some targeted levels of macroeconomic variables can be attained over the long run.

Estimates of the equilibrium exchange rate differ according to the method of model setting and sample period. Therefore, it may be more reliable to judge the present level of the

---

15 For example, the maximum and minimum targets can be set at +3 percent and at −3 percent of GDP, respectively.

16 See Michael R. Rosenberg (1996), Currency Forecasting: A Guide to Fundamental and Technical Models of Exchange Rate Determination, Irwin Professional Publishing, pp. 31−34.

exchange rate based on the equilibrium exchange rates that highly-reputed international organizations or private research institutions publish. Examples of equilibrium exchange rates frequently cited by many analysts and economists are estimates based on the real effective exchange rates (REERs) from the International Monetary Fund and the Bank for International Settlements,[17] and estimates of the fundamental equilibrium exchange rates (FEERs)[18] by Cline and Williamson at the Peterson Institute for International Economics.[19]

According to estimates from the IMF's July 2012 External Sector Report and the IMF's Article IV Consultation with Korea, the real effective exchange rate of the won was moderately undervalued by between zero and ten percent and the won REER was about seven percent below its historical average.[20] The REER indices compiled by BIS showed that

17 IMF compiles real effective exchange rate indices based on relative unit labor costs which are the ratio of total labor costs to real output, while BIS compiles REER indices based on relative consumer prices.

18 The economic concept of fundamental equilibrium exchange rates (FEERs) was first propounded by Williamson (1983). An operational method for arriving at multilaterally consistent estimates of FEERs, that is a symmetric matrix inversion method model (SMIM), was developed by Cline (2008), and has been applied over the past five years in this series of estimates. See Cline and Williamson (2012), "Estimates of Fundamental Equilibrium Exchange Rates," Policy Brief 12–14, May, and "Updated Estimates of Fundamental Equilibrium Exchange Rates," Policy Brief 12–23, Peterson Institute for International Economics, November.

19 The Peterson Institute for International Economics was founded by C. Fred Bergsten 1981 as a private, nonprofit, nonpartisan research institution devoted to the study of international economic policy.

20 See the U.S. Department of the Treasury (2012), "Report to Congress on International Economic and Exchange Rate Policies," November 27.

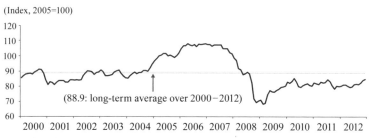

Figure 2.3 Real Effective Exchange Rate Movements in Korea, 2000–2012

(Index, 2005=100)

(88.9: long-term average over 2000–2012)

Source: Bank for International Settlements (BIS).

the won REER was 84.8 as of December 2012, meaning the level of actual exchange rate at that time was undervalued by 4.6 percent relative to long-term average REER (88.9) over 2000–2012.[21] Meanwhile, Cline and Williamson semiannually estimate equilibrium exchange rate levels in major advanced and emerging economies, and then assess the degree to which actual exchange rates deviate from the equilibrium levels. In a paper released on November 2012, Korea's FEER-consistent exchange rate was estimated as 1,080 won against the US dollar, and thus the actual value of Korean won (₩1,106 on October 2012) was undervalued by 2.4 percent against the US dollar. In other emerging economies, the values for the Chinese

21   The current BIS REER indices published with the base year of 2010 were transformed to the indices with the base year of 2005 in this book. It was because macroeconomic variables of 2005, in terms of inflation, economic growth and current account, were more consistent with desirable external and internal balances than those of 2010.

yuan, Hong Kong dollar, Taiwan dollar, Malaysia ringgit, and Singapore dollar were undervalued by 5.9 percent, 12.9 percent, 13.3 percent, 10.2 percent, and 28.5 percent against the US dollar, respectively.

When we make an assessment of the current level of the exchange rate by using estimates of REERs based on IMF and BIS indices or estimates of the FEERs by Cline and Williamson, we have to recall the point that these exchange rates are concepts of the equilibrium exchange rate over the long term. In other words, even though the actual exchange rate may deviate from the long-term equilibrium exchange rate in the short run, it does not necessarily mean that the present exchange rate should be adjusted to the level of long-term equilibrium exchange rate over the near term. But, if the actual exchange rate deviates excessively from the long-term equilibrium exchange rate for a considerable period, it should be borne in mind that it may worsen imbalances in the real economy and financial markets.

On the other hand, the forecast exchange rates or levels of appropriate exchange rates as estimated by major local research institutions or international investment banks may reflect their subjective positions. Therefore, we have to pay attention to this point when we attempt to assess the adequacy of the current level of the exchange rate by employing their estimated exchange rates. Policy makers or economic analysts, however, should refer to their estimated appropriate exchange rates. The forecasts for the average won/dollar rate in 2013 by major local private research institutions were within a range of ₩1,050 – ₩1,093, 3.0 percent to 6.8 percent below the previous

Table 2.5 Outlook for KRW/USD Exchange Rate in 2013,
by Key Economic Research Institutions in Korea[1]

(Won)

KERI	KIF	LGERI	SERI
1,054 (Dec. 2012)	1,052 (Nov. 2012)	1,050 (Dec. 2012)	–
1,065 (Mar. 2013)	1,093 (May. 2013)	1,070 (Apr. 2013)	–

1. Parenthesis indicates the release time of outlook for KRW/USD exchange rate by each institution.
   SERI decided not to disclose a forecast for the KRW/USD exchange rate in 2013.
Sources: Korea Economic Research Institute (KERI); Korea Institute of Finance (KIF); LG
Economic Research Institute (LGERI); Samsung Economic Research Institute (SERI).

year's level (₩1,126.76).

As we have noted above, it is a very difficult job to judge the current level of the exchange rate. It is not perhaps appropriate for me to speak on the adequacy of the present exchange rate, given that I was the Bank of Korea's Director-General in charge of exchange rate policy together with staff from the Ministry of Strategy and Finance not long ago.

General readers, however, have to take into consideration the following points when they assess the adequacy of the current exchange rate. First of all, it is desirable to make an evaluation based on the basis of periods of a quarter, a half or full year rather than at a point in time. This is because quarterly data of variables are used in models for estimating the equilibrium exchange rate, while a target or forecast level of macroeconomic variables is set on an annual basis. Second, they have to judge the current level of the exchange rate by taking into account present economic and financial conditions rather than through direct comparison with the long-term equilibrium exchange rate. It is important to analyze the trend of the exchange rate movements rather than overreacting to it, even though the current level of exchange rate may deviate from the long-term equilibrium exchange rate. In other words, it is more crucial to analyze the trend—whether the present exchange rate diverges from or converges towards the long-term exchange rate. Third, if the present exchange rate deviates from the long-term exchange rate for a long time, there are both negative and positive effects. Generally speaking, if the current level of the exchange rate is higher than the originally expected level, exports will increase more than their target or forecast volume, but prices will rise higher than their target or forecast level. But if the present level of exchange rate is lower than initially forecast, the reverse will occur. Accordingly, both pros and cons should be considered.

Volatility of Exchange Rate

Some media, research institutions and scholars argue strongly that policy authorities have to devise methods for reducing the volatility of the won/dollar exchange rate, pointing out that the won's volatility had been among the highest in the global market following the collapse of Lehman Brothers.

Comparing Won/Dollar Exchange Rate Volatility
with Those of Other Currencies

So how much volatility has the won/dollar exchange rate experienced lately, compared to the past as well as other currencies? There are various ways to measure volatility. This book calculated percentage changes based on the daily market close because it is easier to measure volatility, as well as to make international comparisons. Volatility in the won/dollar rate increased 7.6 times from 0.22 percent in 2007 to 1.67 percent during the period of September 2008 through March 2010, in the wake of Lehman Brothers' collapse. Since then, it has quickly declined, falling to 0.29 percent in 2012, though still relatively high compared to 2007.

The volatility of other currencies after Lehman Brothers' collapse also jumped sharply, apart from countries with managed floating or fixed exchange rate regimes. In particular, currency volatility in Australia and Brazil, where the size of the economy is similar to that of Korea, was higher than that of the won/dollar rate, during the Lehman Brothers crisis. Currency volatility in Poland and Hungary has also been greater than in Korea on the whole. In 2012, the volatility of advanced economies' currencies was also greater than that of the Korean won.

While it is true that Korean won's volatility after Lehman Brothers' collapse increased significantly, the degree of volatility was not the highest in the world as some media and research institutions and scholars have claimed.

Table 2.6 Trends of Interday Exchange Rate Volatility[1]
in Selected Countries

(Average of daily percentage changes during the period, percent)

	2007	2008	Sep. 2008 – Mar. 2009	2009	2010	2011	2012
KRW/USD[2]	0.22	0.99	1.67	0.71	0.60	0.51	0.29
JPY/USD[3]	0.44	0.68	0.92	0.68	0.48	0.37	0.36
USD/EUR[4]	0.30	0.64	0.90	0.61	0.58	0.55	0.40
USD/GBP[5]	0.33	0.61	0.96	0.66	0.50	0.42	0.30
USD/AUD[4]	0.56	1.10	1.70	0.93	0.67	0.68	0.44
CNY/USD[6]	0.09	0.11	0.09	0.02	0.06	0.10	0.10
HKD/USD[6]	0.03	0.02	0.02	0.01	0.03	0.03	0.01
TWD/USD[6]	0.10	0.26	0.31	0.23	0.21	0.22	0.14
SGD/USD[6]	0.19	0.33	0.47	0.30	0.28	0.33	0.25
THB/USD[6]	0.18	0.24	0.27	0.16	0.16	0.24	0.21
MYR/USD[6]	0.20	0.30	0.36	0.35	0.38	0.34	0.30
INR/USD[6]	0.22	0.42	0.56	0.38	0.35	0.34	0.44
MEN/USD[5]	0.30	0.64	1.22	0.76	0.53	0.65	0.53
BRL/USD[5]	0.64	1.16	1.80	0.91	0.63	0.67	0.47
PLN/USD[5]	0.47	0.94	1.61	1.15	0.93	0.94	0.71
HUF/USD[5]	0.51	0.98	1.48	1.09	0.94	1.00	0.76

1. Based on day-on-day rates of change, i.e., [absolute value of (closing rate for day – closing rate for previous day)/closing rate for previous day] × 100.
2. Based on the closing rate in the Seoul foreign exchange market.
3. Based on the rates at 15:00 in the Tokyo foreign exchange market posted by Reuters.
4. Based on the rates at 16:30 in the New York foreign exchange market posted by Reuters.
5. Based on the rates at 17:00 in the New York foreign exchange market posted by Bloomberg.
6. Based on the rates at 20:00 in the Tokyo foreign exchange market posted by Bloomberg.
Sources : Bank of Korea; Reuters; Bloomberg.

Reasons for High Volatility

Frequently, many research institutions and scholars recommend that the Korean won's high volatility ought to be mitigated. But most of them have not presented any effective methods.

The Korean won's high volatility, especially during the foreign currency liquidity crisis was basically ascribed to an unbalanced foreign exchange market due to frequent inflows and outflows of foreign exchange, one-sided transactions under a free-floating exchange rate regime and an open capital market.

First, Korea's exchange rate regime is different from those of other emerging countries. It adopted a free-floating exchange rate regime in December 1997. Subsequently, the daily band on exchange rate fluctuation was abolished, and capital markets have been almost completely opened to foreigners. For these reasons, it has been virtually impossible to maintain daily exchange rate fluctuations within a narrow band. In contrast, China fixed the yuan/dollar rate at CNY6.8388 from end-July of 2008 to 18 June 2010. Even though China decided to move to a more flexible exchange rate from 19 June 2010, the pace of yuan appreciation has been slow and moderate. Hong Kong adopted a currency board system,[22] and Singapore operates an exchange rate targeting system. Malaysia and Thailand have also managed-floating exchange rate regimes. As such, Korea seems to have fewer ways than other emerging economies to intervene in foreign exchange markets.

---

22 The Hong Kong dollar has been linked to the US dollar under a currency arrangement, the Linked Exchange Rate System (LERS), since October 1983 at a rate of HK$7.8/US$1.

Second, the openness of Korea's capital market is relatively high, compared with those of other emerging economies. For international comparison, we generally refer to Capital Access Indexes from the Milken Institute[23] and Investment Freedom Index at the Wall Street Journal and the Heritage Foundation. According to Capital Access Index of 2009, Korea's index score was 7.39, ranking 12th among 122 countries. It was lower than those of Hong Kong (7.99, second) and Singapore (7.92, fourth), but higher than those of most emerging economies including Malaysia (7.06), Taiwan (6.54), Thailand (6.51), and Mexico (5.50), as well as those of some advanced countries such as France (6.99), Germany (6.84) and Japan (6.72).[24]

Because of the high openness of Korea's capital market, inflows and outflows of foreign capital are frequent. Notably, the weight of foreign investment in total Korean stock market

23   The 2009 Capital Access Index ranks 122 countries for which sufficient data were available. Fifty-six variables are assessed across seven components of each country's economic, financial, and social infrastructures—macroeconomic environment, institutional environment, financial and banking institutions, equity market development, bond market development, alternative sources of capital, and international funding. The Capital Access Index is a composite index of them, which determines the country's overall position. The scores can range from zero to ten, lowest to highest in terms of capital access. See Capital Access Index 2009, Milken Institute, April 2010.

24   Index of Economic Freedom is weighted, based on ten components of economic freedom, assigning a grade in each using a scale from 0 to 100, where 100 represents the maximum freedom. The Investment Freedom is one of ten components. The Investment Freedom Index of 2013 showed similar results to the Capital Access of Milken Institute as a whole. But Germany's score of Investment Freedom Index, 85.0 was higher than Korea's (70.0). See 2013 Index of Economic Freedom, The Heritage Foundation and The Wall Street Journal, January 2013.

Table 2.7 Foreigners' Share of Total Stock Market Capitalization by Country

(Billions of US dollars)

	Market capitalization of listed stocks (A)	Holdings of foreign investors (B)	B/A (%)	As of period-end
Korea	1,178.2 (992.7)	381.8 (302.6)	32.4 (30.5)	2012 (2011)
China	3,412.1	211.4	6.2	2011
Singapore	598.3	116.7	19.5	2011
Malaysia	395.6	66.8	16.9	2011
H.K.	2,258.0	334.4	14.8	2011
Thailand	268.5	69.5	25.9	2011
Mexico	408.7	129.3	31.6	2011
Brazil	1,228.9	351.1	28.6	2011
Austrailia	1,198.2	318.3	26.6	2011

Sources: Bank of Korea; World Federation of Exchanges; IMF; Bank of Thailand; Department of Statistics, Malaysia.

capitalization was 32.4 percent as of the end of 2012, much higher than those in other emerging economies, and slightly higher than in Brazil, Mexico and Australia.

Third, Korea's dependency on short-term foreign currency borrowings through foreign bank branches has been very high, and mobility of foreign capital have been frequent, as shown in Figure 2.4. The total short-term foreign currency debt of

foreign bank branches was 36.1 billion dollars as of the end
of 2012, accounting for 57.9 percent of their overall foreign
currency debt and 28.5 percent of Korea's total external short-
term borrowings. Foreign bank branches mainly use the foreign
currency funds raised through short-term borrowings in FX
swaps and currency swaps with local banks. They have earned
risk-free arbitrage profits by investing the won funds exchanged
against US dollar funds through swap transactions into won-
denominated Treasury Bonds and Monetary Stabilization
Bonds, which can easily be liquidated and have been issued
at higher interest rates than Treasuries from the US or the
eurozone. The high volatility of capital flows involving foreign

Figure 2.4 Changes in Short-term External Debt of
Foreign Bank Branches, 2006–2012

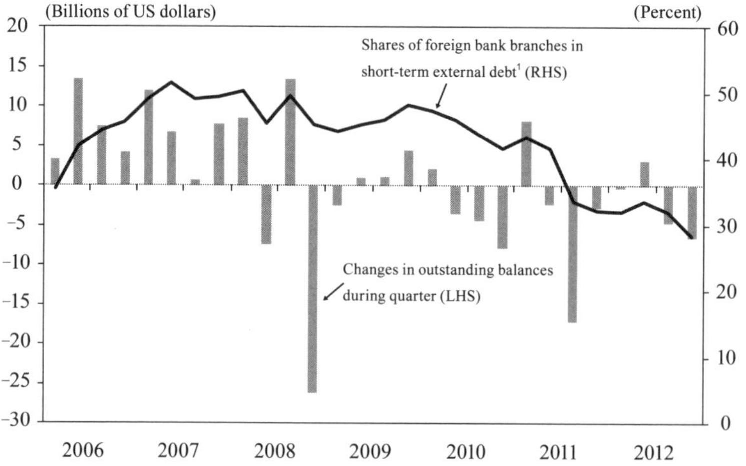

1. Based on outstanding balances at quarter-ends; Short-term external debt of foreign bank branches/
   Total short-term external debt (%).
Source: BOK, Economic Statistics System (ECOS).

bank branches is because their business strategy is affected by the funding conditions of their head offices or changes in the global credit market. In addition, this is partly because foreign bank branches for long raised foreign currency funds and invested them freely, unlike local banks, as a result of their not being subject to the application of foreign currency liquidity ratios.

Fourth, Korea faces very unique geopolitical risks. Whenever military tensions erupt such as the sinking of a South Korea naval frigate or the shelling of Yeonpyeong Island by North Korea in 2010, won/dollar rate volatility surged temporarily.

How Do We Reduce Exchange Rate Volatility?

Alleviating the volatility of their exchange rates is a key policy task for almost all emerging economies, particularly those with free-floating exchange rate regimes, at a period when major advanced countries are maintaining low interest rates and quantitative easing policies over the long term. Solutions to this difficult issue may lie with the 'impossible trinity' or 'trilemma.'[25] This concept refers to the inability to achieve the following three goals at one and the same time: monetary independence, financial integration, and exchange rate stability. Under an autonomous monetary policy system, a country must regulate capital mobility, or it has to impose the daily fluctuation band

---

25 See Aizenman, Chinn, & Ito (2008), "Assessing the emerging global financial architecture: measuring the trilemma's configurations over time," NBER working paper 14533, December.

in order to stabilize exchange rates. As Korea is a member of the OECD, however, the country cannot easily reverse capital liberalization. Also, restricting the daily range of exchange rate fluctuations is difficult because of the country's open capital market.

In light of these points, volatility has been quite high in Korea, compared with other emerging economies with managed floating exchange rate regimes. Such excessive volatility creates a sense of instability among market participants, and makes it difficult for corporations to establish their business targets including investment planning. Furthermore, it will have negative effects on economic growth and price stability. Therefore, policy should be focused on easing excessive volatility, while there ought to be inducements for market participants to absorb a certain degree of the volatility through efforts such as exchange rate risk hedging. In other words, policy makers should elaborate the methods for easing imbalance in foreign exchange supply and demand, even while maintaining the basic framework of the free-floating exchange rate regime and capital liberalization.

It is most important to alleviate the volatility of inflows and outflows of foreign capital. To accomplish this, policy authorities need to devise appropriate methods to limit inflows rather than to control outflows of foreign capital. This is because inflows of hot money or short-term speculative capital tend to lead to a surge of outflows after profit-taking. First of all, policy makers have to make an effort not to create arbitrage opportunities, such as exchange gains, by avoiding the excessive deviation of price variables from target levels through the stable conduct of macroeconomic policy. This will contribute to preventing booms and busts of the economy. Recently, Korea prepared several instruments to curb inflows through the introduction of foreign exchange forward position limits, withdrawal of tax exemptions on foreigners' bond investment income, and the imposition of a foreign exchange macro-prudential stability levy. In the weeks ahead, policy makers should continue these efforts to improve structural and institutional factors behind the mismatch of supply and demand in the foreign exchange market. For example, the foreign currency liquidity ratio, maturity mismatch ratio and the ratio of long-term foreign currency financing to long-term foreign currency loans cannot easily be applied to foreign bank branches at the same levels as domestic banks in the short term, but this issue should be thoroughly reviewed from a long-term viewpoint.

On the other hand, some people advocate that the policy authorities should intervene in foreign exchange market frequently to lessen exchange rate volatility. In other words, this would means policy authorities assuming a selling position when the won/dollar exchange rate jumps, and taking a buying position when it falls substantially. I believe this argument arises because they choose to ignore the fact that Korea has formally abolished the daily band on exchange rates fluctuation, or they have misunderstood the essence of a free-floating exchange rate regime. Exchange rate policies in major countries are regularly monitored by the US Treasury[26] and the IMF. As such, frequent

---

26 The Secretary of the Treasury should submit semiannual reports on the

intervention to maintain exchange rate movements within a narrow range rather than smoothing operations to calm sharp fluctuations can risk denunciation by the international community including the US. Moreover, repeated buying and selling by policy authorities may actually exacerbate exchange rate volatility by confusing market participants or by distorting the price mechanism. In light of these considerations, the case for frequent intervention by the policy authorities to alleviate exchange rate volatility seems unpersuasive.

Some argue low volatility is good. The insistence does not seem to be valid for the following reasons. If the volatility is kept artificially low by a narrow range of daily fluctuations, it will be difficult to absorb changes in the domestic financial and economic situation or withstand shocks from international financial markets. That is, when foreign capital flows out due to deterioration in financial and economic conditions at home and abroad, the pace of outflows will increase. Conversely, when foreign capital flows in, expecting favorable conditions, the pace of inflows is likely to accelerate to reap exchange gains. In addition, maintaining low exchange rate volatility will hinder the creation of various financial products for exchange rate risk hedging, and the progress of financial and foreign exchange markets. Besides this, local financial institutions and enterprises will make fewer efforts to expand their own capacity to respond

international economic and exchange rate policies of the major trading partners of the United States to Congress, pursuant to the Omnibus Trade and Competitiveness Act of 1988. See "Report to Congress on International Economic and Exchange Rate Policies," US Department of the Treasury, 27 November 2012.

to exchange rate volatility, thus falling into the moral hazard of depending on policy authorities alone.

Relationship between Interest Rates and the Exchange Rate

Some people insist that if the Bank of Korea lowers its policy rate under current conditions, this will put upward pressure on the won/dollar rate (won depreciation) by decreasing inflows of foreign capital through the narrowing of the gap between domestic and international interest rates.

We cannot conclusively say that this insistence is always right. There are times when a decline in the benchmark interest rate brings about a fall in the won/dollar exchange rate (won appreciation). If we examine policy rate and exchange rate movements since 2000 in Korea, it is difficult to find a consistent relationship between the two. Policy rates were raised on 16 occasions between February 2000 and June 2011. The won/dollar exchange rate fell on ten of those occasions, but rebounded the following day on six of those occasions. Unexpectedly, the won/dollar exchange rate increased on six occasions. Conversely, the policy rates were reduced on 17 occasions between February 2001 and May 2013. The exchange rate rose on ten of those occasions, but fell the next day on six of those occasions. Moreover, the won/dollar rate decreased on seven occasions.

Why were the results at times different from those argued above? We can find the reasons for the divergence from the following two perspectives. First, the argument above is based

Table 2.8 Increases in BOK Policy Interest Rate and Changes in KRW/USD Exchange Rate

Date	Changes in policy rate (% APR)	Changes in KRW/USD rate (%)		
		On the day[1]	On next day[2]	End-the month[3]
10 Feb. 2000	+25bp (4.75 → 5.00)	−0.20	−0.49	0.70
5 Oct. 2000	+25bp (5.00 → 5.25)	−0.13	−0.21	1.71
5 Jul. 2002	+25bp (4.00 → 4.25)	−0.13	0.46	−4.29
11 Oct. 2005	+25bp (3.25 → 3.50)	0.38	0.11	0.22
8 Dec. 2005	+25bp (3.50 → 3.75)	−0.10	−0.05	−2.30
9 Feb. 2006	+25bp (3.75 → 4.00)	0.20	−0.50	0.01
8 Jun. 2006	+25bp (4.00 → 4.25)	0.55	0.10	0.07
10 Aug. 2006	+25bp (4.25 → 4.50)	−0.17	0.41	0.21
12 Jul. 2007	+25bp (4.50 → 4.75)	−0.10	−0.15	0.01
9 Aug. 2007	+25bp (4.75 → 5.00)	−0.14	0.98	1.53
7 Aug. 2008	+25bp (5.00 → 5.25)	0.06	1.12	7.20
9 Jul. 2010	+25bp (2.00 → 2.25)	0.50	0.87	−2.20
16 Nov. 2010	+25bp (2.25 → 2.50)	−0.21	1.36	2.46
13 Jan. 2011	+25bp (2.50 → 2.75)	−0.46	0.05	0.19
10 Mar. 2011	+25bp (2.50 → 2.75)	0.56	0.21	−1.69
10 Jun. 2011	+25bp (2.50 → 2.75)	−0.03	0.30	−1.40

1. Indicates percentages change from the previous day to the day when BOK Base Rate was changed, based on closing KRW/USD rate in the Seoul foreign exchange market. Figures of (+) or (−) represent rates of depreciation or appreciation of the won against the US dollar, respectively.
2. Indicates percentage change from closing KRW/USD rate of the day when BOK Base Rate was changed to closing KRW/USD rate of the next business day.
3. Indicates percentage change from closing KRW/USD rate of the day before BOK Base Rate was changed to last day of the month.

Source: Bank of Korea, Economic Statistics System (ECOS)

Table 2.9 Decreases in BOK Policy Interest Rate and Changes in KRW/USD Exchange Rate

Date	Changes in policy rate (% APR)	Changes in KRW/USD rate (%)		
		On the day[1]	On next day[2]	End-the month[3]
8 Feb. 2001	−25bp (5.25→5.00)	0.09	−0.31	−1.07
5 Jul. 2001	−25bp (5.00→4.75)	0.10	−0.20	0.36
9 Aug. 2001	−25bp (4.75→4.50)	0.26	−0.38	−0.54
19 Sep. 2001	−50bp (4.50→4.00)	−0.03	0.08	0.98
13 May. 2003	−25bp (4.25→4.00)	0.37	0.05	0.90
10 Jul. 2003	−25bp (4.00→3.75)	−0.06	−0.02	0.05
12 Aug. 2004	−25bp (3.75→3.50)	−0.19	0.41	−0.58
11 Nov. 2004	−25bp (3.50→3.25)	0.14	−0.68	−5.61
9 Oct. 2008	−25bp (5.25→5.00)	−1.11	−5.11	−7.46
27 Oct. 2008	−75bp (5.00→4.25)	1.44	1.75	−9.21
7 Nov. 2008	−25bp (4.25→4.00)	−0.17	−0.19	10.37
11 Dec. 2008	−100bp (4.00→3.00)	−2.53	1.03	−9.64
9 Jan. 2009	−50bp (3.00→2.50)	0.75	1.19	3.49
12 Feb. 2009	−50bp (2.50→2.00)	0.79	−0.02	10.08
12 Jul. 2012	−25bp (3.25→3.00)	0.93	−0.10	−0.90
11 Oct. 2012	−25bp (3.00→2.75)	−0.03	−0.28	−2.14
9 May. 2013	−25bp (2.75→2.50)	0.41	1.38	3.55

The indications of 1, 2, and 3 are the same as those in table 2.8.

Source: Bank of Korea, Economic Statistics System (ECOS).

on the assumption that interest rate movements affect only foreigners' local bond investments.

According to exchange rate determination theories such as the balance of payments flow approach, monetary approach, and portfolio approach,[27] a decline in the local interest rate acts to depreciate the won against the US dollar by decreasing inflows of foreign capital, based on a recognition of capital mobility as a major factor in exchange rate determination. These approaches claim that a decline in the local interest rate decreases inflows of foreign capital by reducing the differential between domestic and foreign interest rates, assuming the bond market is the only object of foreign capital mobility. If, however, we include the equity market as an object of foreign capital mobility, then the effect of lower interest rates may vary.

Therefore, the effect of interest rates on exchange rates through capital mobility should be analyzed via foreigners' bond investments, foreigners' equity investments and overseas borrowings by local banks. As it is well known, lower interest rates lead to a higher exchange rate through the channel of bond investment inflows as expected yields on bond investments fall. The overseas borrowings channel also has a similar effect. But in the equity investment channel a decrease in the policy rate acts to bring about a fall in the exchange rate by inducing inflows of equity investment funds due to the rise in expected yields on equity investments arising from an expected expansion

27 See Michael R. Rosenberg (1996), Currency Forecasting: A Guide to Fundamental and Technical Models of Exchange Rate Determination, Irwin Professional Publishing, pp. 68–207.

of economic activity.

To sum up, the effect of lower policy rates or market interest rates on exchange rates via capital flows depends on the relative size of the equity investment channel (downward pressure on the exchange rate) versus the sum of the bond investment and overseas borrowings channels combined (upward pressure on the exchange rate) as in Figure 2.5. That is, if the size of the equity investment channel is greater than the sum of the bond investment channel and overseas borrowings channel, a decline in interest rates will bring about a lower exchange rate (currency appreciation). In the reverse case, a decrease in policy rate or market rates may result in a rise in exchange rate (currency depreciation).

Which channel is greater depends on the economic and financial conditions at the time. If monetary policy still adopts a tightening stance even after the interest rate cut, then foreign equity investments are likely to continue to flow out or stop flowing in. This implies the local currency is likely to depreciate further. Conversely, if monetary policy is still accommodative or expansionary even after a cut in the policy rate, then foreigners' equity investment funds will flow in due to the expected economic expansion. In emerging market economies, particularly, the value of the local currency is likely to appreciate because the effect of foreigners' equity investments is expected to be larger than that of foreigners' bond investments. So it is difficult to conclude that a decline in interest rates will necessarily bring about local currency depreciation because overall economic and financial conditions at the time need to be considered.

Figure 2.5 Impact of BOK Policy Rate Change on the KRW/USD Exchange Rate through Investment Channels

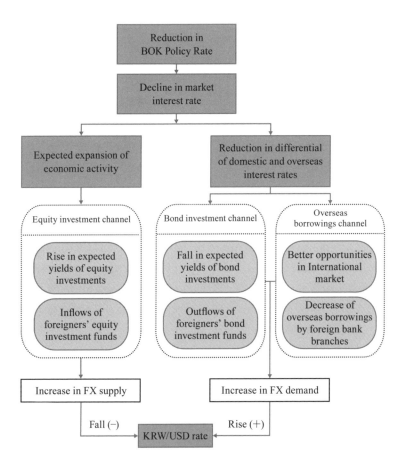

In addition, even after review of the results of foreign empirical analysis, the relationship between interest rates and the exchange rate remains unclear. This is especially true in emerging market economies because the openness of the equity market is greater than that of the bond market. Nowadays, the impact of inflows and outflows of equity investment funds on the local exchange rate is growing larger.[28] As such, in the case of decrease in interest rates, we frequently find that the amount of equity investment funds inflows exceeds the amount of bond investment funds outflows, exerting downward pressure on the exchange rate

The second reason that the relationship between interest rates and the exchange rate is not direct is attributed to the fact that the exchange rate is affected by both capital flows and other factors—fluctuations in the differences in current account positions, economic growth rates and inflation rates between two countries, as well as market participants' changing expectations on exchange rates. Accordingly, even though a decline in the policy rate should exert upward pressure on the exchange rate through foreign capital outflow, if factors acting in an opposing direction on capital movements are disclosed or are expected to be announced at around the time of the decrease in policy rate, then the effect of these other factors on exchange rate may be larger than the effect of foreign capital outflows on the exchange rate, eventually leading to an appreciation in the exchange rate.

---

28   See Hau & Rey (2006), "Exchange Rates, Equity Prices and Capital Flows," Review of Financial Studies 19.

Chapter 3

Foreign Currency Liquidity Management

Prior to the currency crisis of 1997, the Bank of Korea regularly provided foreign currency funds to commercial banks through foreign currency deposits and foreign currency loans against the security of export bills. After that crisis, however, the Bank abolished its foreign currency deposit system for commercial banks, maintaining only a foreign currency loan system secured against export bills for emergency use.

Meanwhile, the Bank of Korea participated in the swap market for the first time in September 2007. It introduced a competitive FX swap auction as well as a competitive US dollar loan facility auction, using the US dollar proceeds from currency swaps with the Federal Reserve after the collapse of Lehman Brothers, operating them until August and December 2009, respectively.

This chapter first describes the system of providing foreign currency liquidity to commercial banks by the Bank of Korea. Then, it covers two important related issues—whether to expand the supply of foreign currency liquidity to domestic banking institutions, and the improvement of the swap transaction method to a more market-oriented, competitive swap auction.

1. Foreign Currency Liquidity Supply System at the Bank of Korea

In advanced economies, central banks do not operate a system of supplying foreign currency liquidity such as foreign currency loans to financial institutions during ordinary times. This is because the currencies of advanced economies can be exchanged against other currencies freely at any time in the international financial market. In addition, the liquidity is abundant in advanced foreign exchange markets.

In exceptional cases, central banks provide financial institutions with foreign currency funds. For example, in the wake of the global financial crisis of September 2008, central banks such as the ECB, Bank of England, and Bank of Japan established bilateral swap arrangements with the US Federal Reserve, and then lent local financial institutions substantial US dollar funds obtained through currency swaps with the Fed. Other central banks such as the Reserve Bank of Australia and the Reserve Bank of New Zealand exchange their own currencies against foreign currencies through currency swaps with their local commercial banks, separately from ordinary open market operations, in situations where it is necessary to adjust financial market liquidity.

In Korea, prior to the Asian financial crisis of 1997, the Bank of Korea regularly provided foreign currency funds to commercial banks, such as foreign currency deposits and foreign currency loans against the security of export bills. After the currency crisis, however, sufficient holdings of foreign exchange reserves were widely recognized to be essential.

Therefore, the Bank of Korea abolished its system of foreign currency deposits for commercial banks, maintaining only a system of foreign currency loans secured against export bills for emergency use.

Meanwhile, the Bank of Korea participated for the first time in the swap market in September 2007. It introduced a competitive foreign exchange (FX) swap auction as well as a competitive US dollar loan facility auction, using the proceeds of US dollar swaps with the Federal Reserve after the collapse of Lehman Brothers, operating them until August and December 2009, respectively.

2. FX Swap and Currency Swap

An FX swap and a currency swap are contractual agreements between two parties to exchange cash flows of two different currencies. They are both a form of financial derivatives transaction, where principal amounts of two currencies are exchanged between financial institutions or between financial institutions and corporations at the origination date of the swap contract. Then the principal amounts are again exchanged between them into the original currencies at maturity. These swaps are virtually the same in the sense that counterparties to the swaps exchange two currencies and hedge exchange rate risk during the contract period.

Swaps between the Bank of Korea and financial institutions are the same as the standard swaps described above, but they differ from standard swaps in the purpose of transactions. The former aim to alleviate imbalances in the swap market and to curb excessive inflows of foreign capital in quest of arbitrage gains by reducing arbitrage incentives. After reviewing a standard swap transaction, I will explain the swap transactions between the Bank of Korea and commercial banks.

Standard Type of FX Swap and Currency Swap

Structure of Standard FX Swap

An FX swap is a contractual agreement in which the two parties to the swap exchange fixed amounts of two different currencies, based on the spot exchange rate, on the origination date of the contract (between financial institutions or between financial institutions and enterprises), and then reexchange the principle amounts of the two currencies, based on the contracted exchange rate, at maturity. These swaps are categorized by the types of the combined transactions. A spot-forward swap is a combination of an FX spot transaction and an FX forward transaction. A forward-forward swap is a combination of a short-term FX forward transaction and a long-term FX forward transaction. A spot-spot swap or a backward swap is a combination of two FX spot transactions.[29]

---

29   In the settlement methods of FX spot transactions between commercial banks in which any foreign exchange brokerage company does not intervene, there are "value today," "value tomorrow," and "value spot" which are settled today, tomorrow, and on the second business day following the contract.

In the case of an FX swap, buying and selling are distinguished, based on the transaction on the far date. The buying of an FX swap is referred to as a sell & buy swap, in which one of the parties agrees to sell foreign currency at the near date to the counterparty, and at the same time, to buy the same foreign currency at the far date from the counterparty. On the other hand, the selling of an FX swap is defined as a buy & sell swap, in which one of the parties agrees to buy foreign currency at the near date from the counterparty, and at the same time, to sell foreign currency at the far date to the counterparty. As described above, the FX swap takes the form of buying and selling of foreign exchange, but it is very much similar to the lending and borrowing of short-term funds in the money market, as it allows the borrowing of the necessary currency under the terms of a repurchase agreement in line with provision of a holding currency as collateral during the period of the contract.

An FX swap, in general, is a short-term transaction with a maturity of a year or less. In a swap, interest rate payments between two parties do not occur periodically during the contract period, because the interest rate differential between two currencies is reflected in the exchange rate at maturity when the principal amounts are again exchanged. A swap point is defined as a numerical value which is calculated by subtracting a spot exchange rate on the swap's origination date from a pre-determined exchange rate at maturity (generally the forward exchange rate). A swap rate is calculated by dividing a swap point by a spot exchange rate on the origination date of contract.

The motives for entering into a foreign exchange swap are to raise other currencies, to hedge exchange rate risk, to adjust foreign exchange position, and to acquire arbitrage[30] profits within one-year maturity. In greater detail, the purpose of an FX swap is to balance a surplus or shortage of a currency by raising another currency needed instead of lending out an excess of a currency held in reserve at present. For example, an FX swap is used as a means of raising currencies needed temporarily between local banks that have sufficient Korean won funds but are short of foreign currency funds and foreign bank branches that have foreign currency funds in reserve but need to secure won funds. In addition, swaps are employed to raise foreign currency funds needed to adjust an imbalance in the foreign exchange position of a commercial bank resulting from FX forward transactions with firms. Swaps are also utilized to earn profits without exchange rate risk through arbitrage, which exploits the difference between the interest rate differential and the swap rate of two currencies. For example, if local banks buy FX forwards from export firms, they have to sell FX spot equivalent to the amount to adjust their foreign exchange position. To do this, domestic banks raise necessary foreign currency through an FX swap with foreign bank branches. This permits them to hedge foreign exchange

---

30 Prices are not always simultaneously in equilibrium. That is, one asset or derivative contract is mispriced relative to another. This market inefficiency provides arbitrage opportunities to traders. In arbitrage transactions, traders act to acquire profits arising from difference in prices during times when they are moving to new equilibrium levels. Derivative contracts are generally used for arbitrage.

Figure 3.1 Example of an FX Swap Transaction

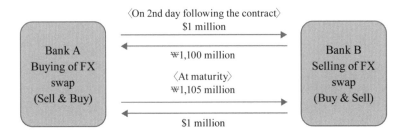

risk through adjustment of their position, while foreign bank branches can acquire arbitrage profits through investments in local bonds.

Figure 3.1 is a cash flow diagram that illustrates the transaction structure of an FX swap. We assume Bank A makes a sell & buy swap contract of one million US dollars with the terms of ₩1,100/$ as a spot exchange rate and ₩1,105/$ as a three-month forward exchange rate with Bank B. Bank A gives one million dollars to Bank B on the second business day following the contract, and receives 1,100 million won (₩1,100 × $1 million) from Bank B. At maturity and on the termination date of the contract, Bank A receives one million dollars back from Bank B, and pays 1,150 million won (₩1,105 × $1 million) to bank. As a result, Bank A and Bank B can secure Korean won funds and US dollar funds in the short term.

Figure 3.2 is a cash flow diagram that illustrates an arbitrage of employing a three-month FX swap. With an inflow of US dollar funds to Korea, a foreign investor (or a foreign bank branch) exchanges the dollar funds with Korean won funds

Figure 3.2 Example of Arbitrage through a Three-Month FX Swap

⇒ Arbitrage profits = Yield on MSB (2.78%) – LIBOR (0.31%) – Swap rate (2.14%)
　　　　　　　　　= 0.33%p APR (based on end-2012)

——————▶ flow of principal amount

··············▶ flow of interest payments

through sell & buy swaps with local banks, and then buys the Monetary Stabilization Bonds in the local financial market. Upon maturity, the foreign investor receives the principal amount with interest (2.78% APR) in Korean won, and then the foreign investor reexchanges the won funds into dollar funds at the three-month forward exchange rate stated in the contract. At the same time, the foreign investor returns the dollar funds to the lender and pays the interest (three-month LIBOR, 0.31% APR). As a result, the foreign investor gets profits (0.33% APR) equivalent to the "interest rate on Korean bonds (2.78% APR) – interest rate on borrowed dollar funds (LIBOR, 0.31% APR) – swap rate (2.14% APR)."

Structure of Standard Currency Swap

Like an FX swap, a currency swap is a contractual agreement, in which two parties to the swap exchange fixed amounts of two different currencies on the origination date between financial institutions or between financial institutions and firms, and then reexchange the principals in the two currencies at maturity. In a currency swap, the exchange rate on the origination date of the contract is the same as that at maturity, and interest payments are periodically exchanged between the parties during the contract period. By type, there is a fixed-fixed currency swap in which the fixed interest rates on two different currencies are exchanged, a cross-currency coupon swap in which a fixed interest rate and a floating interest rate are exchanged, and a cross-currency basis swap in which a floating interest rate and a floating interest rate are exchanged. A cross-currency coupon swap is the most common type, and is explained below.

In a currency swap, a "currency swap pay" is a transaction in which one of the parties (i.e., a currency swap payer) pays the amount of the principal in a foreign currency to the counterparty and, at the same time, receives the equivalent amount in Korean won from the counterparty on the swap's origination date, and does a reverse trade at maturity. On the contrary, a "currency swap receive" is a transaction in which one of the parties (i.e., a currency swap receiver) receives the amount of principal in a foreign currency from the counterparty and, at the same time, pays the equivalent amount in Korean won from the counterparty on the swap's origination date, and then does a reverse trade at maturity. Therefore, a currency swap pay and a currency swap receive are similar concepts to a sell & buy swap and a buy & sell swap, respectively.

A currency swap and an FX swap are the same in the sense that both are a buying and selling transaction with the features of repurchase agreements. But they are different in the swap period, the contracted exchange rate, and the method of interest rate exchange.

In more detail, the maturity of an FX swap is a short term of one year or less, while the maturity of a currency swap is a longer term of one year or more. In a currency swap, the exchange rates applied on the origination date and at maturity are the same. In an FX swap, however, the exchange rates between the two currencies on the origination date and at maturity are different because the interest rate differential between the two currencies is reflected in the exchange rate at maturity, taking into account the maturity of the swap. Due to the differences of methods in applying exchange rates in an FX swap and a currency swap, interest rates on the principals swapped in the two currencies are not exchanged in the former, whereas they are exchanged every six (or three) months in the latter. In a currency swap, a swap rate between Korean won funds and US dollar funds is expressed as a fixed interest rate, which is called a currency swap rate (CRS rate). A currency swap payer pays a CRS rate to a currency swap receiver, and receives a floating US dollar rate (for example, London Interbank Offered Rate with six month maturities) from a currency swap receiver. An FX swap and a currency swap are transacted directly by two parties or through foreign exchange brokerage companies.

One difference in the transaction motives for an FX swap and a currency swap is that the maturity in the latter is a long term of one year or more, whereas the maturity in the former is short. Other transaction motives, such as raising other currencies, hedging exchange rate risks, adjusting foreign exchange positions, and acquiring arbitrage profits, are the same for both swaps. In particular, local banks that buy FX forwards with maturities of one year or more from shipbuilders make currency swap contracts with foreign bank branches and local firms to adjust foreign exchange positions and to hedge exchange rate risks. Local banks also enter into currency swap contracts as an alternative to raising foreign currency funds in case it is difficult to borrow long-term foreign funds or when interest rates of foreign fund borrowings increase.

Figure 3.3 is a cash flow diagram that illustrates the transaction structure of a currency swap. We suppose Bank A makes a currency swap contract of one million US dollars with Bank B, based on an exchange rate of ₩1,100/$ on the origination date and at maturity. The currency swap has three stages for cash flow exchanges. First, on the second business day following the contract, Bank A gives one million dollars

Figure 3.3 Example of a Currency Swap

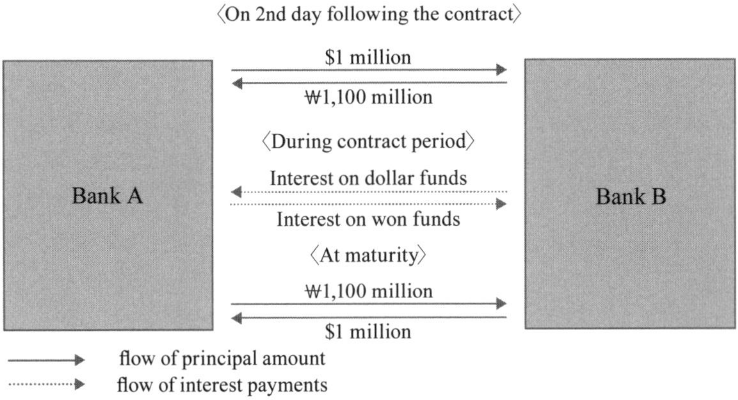

⟨On 2nd day following the contract⟩

Bank A	$1 million →	Bank B
	← ₩1,100 million	
	⟨During contract period⟩	
	Interest on dollar funds ←	
	→ Interest on won funds	
	⟨At maturity⟩	
	₩1,100 million →	
	← $1 million	

⟶ flow of principal amount
┄┄┄▶ flow of interest payments

to Bank B and receives 1,100 million won (₩1,100 × $1 million) from Bank B. In the second stage, interest payments are periodically swapped during the contract period. Bank A pays the interest (CRS rate) on won funds to Bank B every six months, and at the same time, receives the interest on dollar funds from Bank B. In the third and last stage, Bank A receives one million dollars from Bank B and gives 1,100 million won (₩1,100 × $1 million) to Bank B.

In the meantime, a currency swap for the purpose of profit-taking is made when a difference exists between the swap rate (CRS rate) and the yield on won-denominated bond. This swap is conducted in case an arbitrageur (in general, a foreign investor) moves to acquire profits by investing won funds, which are exchanged against foreign currency funds raised abroad, into won-denominated bonds.

Figure 3.4 is a cash flow diagram that illustrates the transaction structure of a three-year currency swap with the aim of gaining arbitrage profits. A foreign investor (or a foreign bank branch) borrows US dollar funds abroad, and pays a floating rate (six-month LIBOR) denominated in dollars every six months. In the local swap market, the foreigner exchanges dollar funds with won funds, based on a pre-determined exchange rate, through currency swap contracts with local banks. During the contract period, the foreigner and local bank exchange fixed rate (CRS rate, 1.91% APR) and floating rate (LIBOR) payments every six months, respectively. The foreigner buys local bonds with the won funds, and receives coupons (2.82% APR) on the bonds every six months. Upon maturity, the foreign investor withdraws the principal of bonds,

Figure 3.4 Example of Arbitrage through a Three-Year Currency Swap

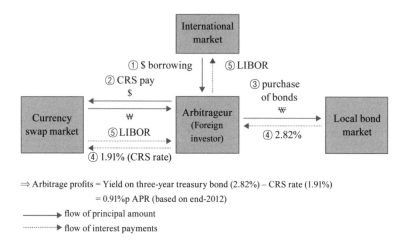

⇒ Arbitrage profits = Yield on three-year treasury bond (2.82%) – CRS rate (1.91%)

= 0.91%p APR (based on end-2012)

———➤ flow of principal amount

·············➤ flow of interest payments

and at the same time, exchanges won funds for dollar funds again. The foreign investor redeems the overseas borrowings with dollar funds received from the local bank. Consequently, the foreign investor receives a gain (0.91% APR) equivalent to the "interest rate on Korean bonds (2.82% APR) − CRS rate (1.91% APR) + interest rate received from the CRS receiver (six-month LIBOR) − interest rate on the dollar-denominated borrowings (six-month LIBOR)" or "interest rate of Korean bonds (2.82% APR) − CRS rate (1.91% APR)."

Bank of Korea's Swap Market Participation and Competitive Swap Auction System

Introduction of Swap Market Participation System

The Bank of Korea's Swap Market Participation System was announced to the general public by the Director-General of the International Department after the Bank participated directly in the swap market for the first time at 17:15 on September 11, 2007. The system has since been operated in consideration of market conditions. Under the system, the Bank of Korea conducts swap transactions with its agent banks, and they, in turn, conduct swap transactions with other commercial banks. The Bank of Korea made the decision to participate directly in the swap market to ease imbalances in the swap market and to curb increases in foreign debt.

Figure 3.5 Structure of Swap Market Participation

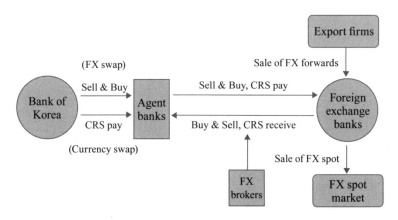

From 2006, forward selling to hedge exchange rate risk grew markedly due to large orders to shipbuilders and a significant expansion in overseas securities investment by local residents. Local banks increased buy & sell swaps and currency swap receives with foreign bank branches to raise foreign currency funds needed for adjustment (i.e., spot selling) of foreign exchange positions caused by their forward buying. As a result, imbalances in the inter-bank swap market persisted and swap rates dropped more than the differentials between domestic and foreign interest rates. Moreover, imbalances in the swap market deepened further with the rapid rise of global credit risk after BNP Paribas, which had suffered big losses due to securities investments related to sub-prime mortgages in the US, stopped repurchasing its funds on 9 August 2007. Accordingly, swap rates dropped far below differentials between domestic and foreign interest rates. The arbitrage incentive for a three-month maturity, calculated by subtracting the swap rate from the differential between domestic and foreign interest rates, increased rapidly from 26 basis points at the end of 2006 to 66 basis points at the end of June 2007, and to 214 basis points at the end of August 2007. This made conditions for gaining arbitrage profits more favorable. Foreign bank branches, which enjoyed advantages in borrowing costs and terms relative to local banks, borrowed foreign currencies from their head offices, and then invested won funds in domestic bonds, after exchanging the interoffice funds for won currencies through sell & buy swaps and currency swap pays. As a result, domestic bond investments by foreigners, such as the Korean branches and head offices of foreign banks, increased sharply.

In line with increased sell & buy swaps by foreign bank branches, which were responding to the persistent demand for buy & sell swaps by local banks in the swap market, external debt expanded significantly. Since 2006, external debt, in particular short-term debt, increased rapidly, and a substantial portion of this came from foreign bank branches. In 2007, foreigners' overseas borrowing for arbitrage were a major factor behind the increase in external debt. The share of short-term external debt on an original maturity basis among total external debt rose from 40.8 percent at the end of 2005 to 50.7 percent at the end of June 2007. The share of the short-term external debt on a remaining maturity basis, similarly, increased from 41.1 percent to 67 percent in the same period.

On 11 September 2007, the Bank of Korea announced that it participated directly in the swap market, and at the same time, suspended its use of currency swaps linked to foreign currency loans with commercial banks, which had been operating since 2005. Its currency swaps with the National Pension Service were also suspended from December 2007. These measures seemed necessary in light of the following: If the Bank of Korea continued to conduct foreign currency loan-linked currency swaps with commercial banks, participating directly in the swap market via agent banks, two different CRS rates might emerge on similar transactions. Moreover, with the Bank of Korea's currency swaps linked to both foreign currency loans and the National Pension Service, its foreign currency assets were locked in over the long term. Thus, there would be a restriction on the swaps' use as reserve assets for external payments at a time of crisis. Meanwhile, along with the expansion of volume in the swap market, the National Pension Service could easily raise foreign currency funds for overseas investment from the swap market.

Introduction of Competitive Swap Auction System

In October 2008, the Bank of Korea introduced a competitive swap auction system. This is for sell & buy swap transactions conducted under terms, such as offered swap points and accepted amount, determined through a competitive bidding method open to all commercial banks. This is different from the swap market participation system operated with limited agent banks. The purpose of introducing the system was to stabilize the foreign currency funds market by supplying foreign currency funds in a predictable and efficient method to commercial banks facing difficulties in raising foreign capital from abroad in the wake of Lehman Brothers' collapse. The Bank of Korea supplied 10.3 billion US dollars to commercial

Figure 3.6 Structure of Competitive Swap Auction

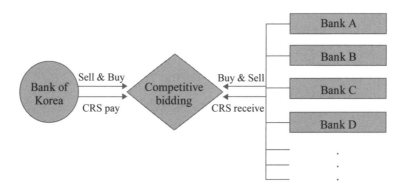

banks through sell & buy swaps using a competitive bidding method on a total of seven occasions between October and December 2007. From the start of 2009, however, conditions underlying foreign currency liquidity in the domestic market showed significant improvements, thanks to a large surplus on the current account, steady inflows of foreign equity investment funds, and favorable foreign currency funding conditions for local banks. Hence, the Bank of Korea began to wind down foreign currency funds provided through sell & buy swaps on a gradual basis whenever contracts matured from 20 January 2009, and withdrew them completely by 8 August 2009. Since then, there have been no sell & buy swap transactions via the competitive bidding method. The Bank of Korea is known to participate in the swap market from time to time in the light of swap market conditions.

3. Foreign Currency Loan System

The Bank of Korea, in principle, has not operated a foreign currency loan system to financial institutions since the currency crisis at end-1997. But, it has extended such loans on a limited basis in case of urgent need.

Introduction of Competitive Bidding Foreign Currency
Loan System

On 30 October 2008, the Bank of Korea announced that it had signed a currency swap agreement with a ceiling of 30 billion dollars with the US Federal Reserve. This facility, like those already established with some ten other central banks, was designed to help improve liquidity conditions in global financial markets and to mitigate the spread of difficulties in obtaining US dollar funding in fundamentally sound and well managed economies. This arrangement was originally authorized through 30 April 2009, but was further extended on two occasions to 1 February 2010.

When comparing the currency swap facility between the Bank of Korea and the Federal Reserve with a standard currency swap between commercial banks, they are the same in the sense that both exchange Korean won and US dollars, and the exchange rates applied between the two currencies on the origination date and at maturity are identical. But the currency swap between the Bank of Korea and the Federal Reserve differs from a standard currency swap in the following aspects. First, the maturity of the former was about three months, whereas the maturity of the latter is typically a year or more. Second, the use of dollar funds raised through currency swaps with the Federal Reserve was restricted to loans for commercial banks, whereas the method of use of the currencies exchanged between two counterparties in the latter case is not limited. Third, the Bank of Korea received interest on the loans at maturity from commercial banks, and then paid the total

Figure 3.7 Structure of Foreign Currency Loans Using US Dollar
Proceeds from Swap Transactions with Fed

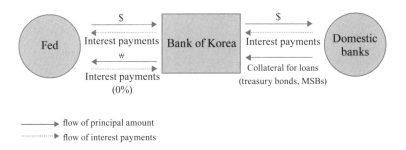

amount to the Federal Reserve immediately. But, because the Federal Reserve deposited the total of the won funds received from the Bank of Korea through the currency swaps in its account with the Bank of Korea, but did not use them, the Bank of Korea did not itself receive interest from the Federal Reserve, nor did it pay interest on these deposits.

On 27 November 2008, the Bank of Korea introduced a system of competitive bidding for foreign currency loans using the US dollar proceeds from swap transactions with the Federal Reserve. Both domestic banks and foreign bank branches were eligible to participate in the competitive auction. Maturity was up to 88 days. The Bank of Korea supplied 16.4 billion dollars to commercial banks on a total of five occasions from 4 December 2008 to 22 January 2009. The loans, however, were wound down on a gradual basis from 19 March 2009, and were collected in full by December 17 that year. As the temporary currency swap arrangement between the Bank of Korea and the Federal Reserve expired on 1 February 2009, the system of competitive bidding for foreign currency loans using the US dollar proceeds from swap transactions with the Federal Reserve was completely halted. The temporary currency swap arrangements between the Federal Reserve and 14 other central banks helped the global financial system stabilize rapidly.

Export Bill Secured Foreign Currency Loan System

In October 1975, the Bank of Korea introduced a foreign currency loan system offering commercial banks foreign currency loans against the security of export bills issued to them by small-and medium-sized companies. This system operated until 1987 and was suspended for about 10 years, until it was temporarily reinstated between May 1998 and September 1999 to support small-and medium-sized companies facing difficulties in raising foreign currency funds due to the currency crisis.

On 11 November 2008, the Bank of Korea again reinstated the system within a limit of 10 billion US dollars to help small and medium-sized companies acquire export financing. The 150 million dollars in loans secured by export bills was released between December 2008 and February 2009. The loans, however, were wound down on a gradual basis from March and were completely withdrawn by July of that year. Since then, the system has ceased operating as commercial banks do not need the loans. The size of foreign currency loans secured against export bills supplied by the Bank of Korea was relatively small. This was because commercial banks had enough scope to use export financing as the government had already supplied five billion dollars of export financing for small-and medium-sized firms to commercial banks through the Export-Import Bank in October 2008, and an additional six billion dollars was in the pipe-line.

4. Key Discussion Points

Two important issues can be raised in regard to the supply of foreign currency liquidity by policy authorities. One is related to the argument that it is necessary for policy authorities to expand the supply of foreign currency liquidity to domestic financial institutions. The other is related to the notion that it is necessary to use market-oriented methods when policy authorities provide foreign currency liquidity.

Argument on Expansion of Foreign Currency Liquidity Supply

Some people have insisted that policy authorities should provide domestic financial institutions with foreign currency liquidity even under normal conditions, and further expand the volume, based on developments in foreign currency funds market. Why this insistence? Their rationale is thought to be based not only on their estimation that the volume of official foreign exchange reserves at present is larger than appropriate, but also on the recognition that policy authorities can increase foreign exchange reserves by withdrawing their foreign currency assets supplied to domestic financial institutions immediately if a financial crisis breaks out. This argument fails to persuade.

First, even though the volume of foreign exchange reserves at present is larger than adequate, they are emergency funds to be used at a time of unexpected crisis. For this reason, it is desirable that policy authorities hold sufficient foreign exchange reserves rather than use them to support financial institutions during ordinary times. This will be examined in detail in Chapter 4, Foreign Exchange Reserve Management.

This is better understood if we recall the economic and financial situations during the Asian financial crisis in 1997 and the global financial crisis of 2008. Some insist that even though policy authorities provide local financial institutions with funds from foreign exchange reserves, the volume does not decrease. Foreign exchange reserves are defined as foreign currency assets that are invested abroad by the monetary authorities and readily available to be turned into spot cash. Thus, if policy authorities provide financial institutions with some of the foreign exchange reserves, the volume of usable reserves is reduced by that amount.

Second, if a financial crisis breaks out, it is actually impossible for domestic financial institutions to withdraw or sell foreign currency assets invested domestically or overseas as we saw in September 2008. Financial institutions cannot take foreign currency loans back from borrowers until the expiration of the contracts, while firms are hard pressed to raise foreign currency funds due to deteriorating borrowing conditions.

Financial institutions would also find it difficult to sell bonds and equity holdings, due to the heavy losses they would incur. Therefore, it does not seem reasonable to argue that the Bank of Korea would be able to rebuild the foreign exchange reserves, because financial institutions would redeem their foreign currency borrowings from the Bank through the sale of foreign asset holdings immediately if a financial crisis breaks out.

Third, domestic financial institutions have to steadily raise their capacity to borrow and operate foreign currency funds, taking into account factors including cost and profit, based on the principle of self responsibility. Expanding this capability is also necessary for domestic financial companies to secure international competitiveness. Various ways to raise foreign funds have already been available to domestic financial institutions. They can secure foreign currency funds through direct borrowings or the issuance of bonds overseas. In addition, because there is sufficient foreign currency liquidity in the domestic FX and swap markets, domestic financial institutions and firms can acquire foreign currency funds through the buying of foreign currencies or the exchange of won funds for foreign currencies after they first raise won-denominated funds.

Fourth, in no country that shares a similar status to Korea in the world economy and international financial markets do central banks provide domestic financial institutions with foreign currency funds under normal conditions. But some other central banks such as the Reserve Bank of Australia and the Reserve Bank of New Zealand do conduct swap transactions that exchange their own currencies against foreign currencies with local commercial banks, in case it is necessary to adjust financial market liquidity.

Given the points above, it is not desirable for policy authorities to use official foreign exchange reserves to provide domestic financial institutions with foreign currency funds during ordinary times. But, in the event of excessive imbalances in the foreign currency funds market persisting, the policy authorities should ease them through increased FX swaps because they are responsible for maintaining financial market stability.

Why Has an Imbalance of Foreign Currency Funds Market Persisted for Such a Long Time?

Let us examine in detail why an imbalance in foreign currency funds has persisted for such a long time and what problems it has caused. First, we need to think about what an imbalance in foreign currency funds market means. The foreign currency funds market in this book refers to a market in which foreign currency funds and Korean won funds are exchanged for a fixed period, that is, an FX swap market and a currency swap market as described above. An imbalance in the swap market means that buy & sell FX swaps (or CRS receives) exceed sell & buy FX swaps (or CRS pays). In other words, the demand for foreign currency funds in the swap market is larger than the supply of foreign currency funds.

Based on interest rate parity conditions, if the differential between domestic and overseas interest rates persists at a positive level, foreign capital has to flow continuously into the domestic bond market. This will ultimately eliminate the incentive for profit-taking on the interest differential by increasing the swap rate through a decline in the spot exchange rate. Actually, however, even in the event that forward exchange rates are higher than spot exchange rates, the phenomenon that swap rates are unable to cover the differential between domestic and overseas interest rates has persisted for a long time. Eventually, an imbalance in the swap market occurs when swap rates are lower than the differential between domestic and overseas interest rates.

What is the reason for this persistent phenomenon? Swap market imbalances have expanded since 2007. Arbitrage incentives for three-year currency swaps increased significantly

Figure 3.8 Movements in CRS Rate, Interest Rate of MSBs and Arbitrage Incentive, 2005–2012

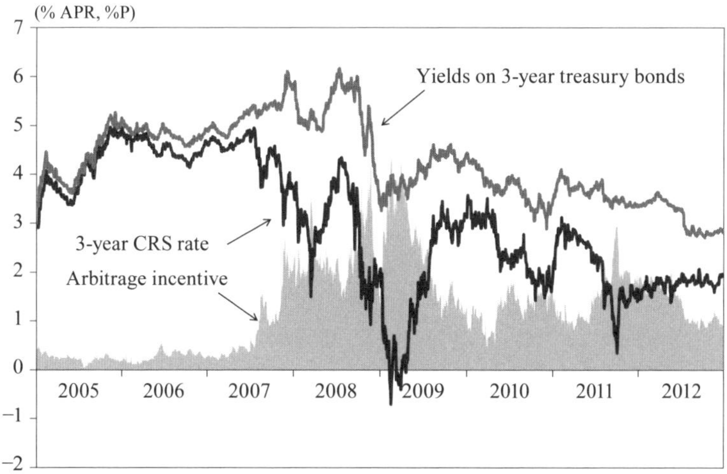

Source: Bank of Korea.

from 29 basis points in 2006 to 82 basis points in 2007 and 233 basis points in both 2008 and 2009.

There are two reasons for this.[31] The first is because of the chronic oversold structure of the swap market, with the selling of FX forwards by export firms and asset management companies being much larger than the buying of FX forwards. This incongruity worsened in 2007 as forwards selling increased greatly due to unprecedented overseas orders by shipbuilders and a sharp increase in foreign bond investments by locals. Shipbuilders sold massive quantities of foreign exchange equivalent to the substantial volume of total orders in the FX forward market to hedge exchange rate risk immediately after they took orders, considering the fact that it takes about three years from order receipt to handover of the ship. Domestic asset management companies also hedged exchange rate risk by selling FX forwards equivalent to the large volume of foreign bond investments by locals. Combined orders for the eight largest shipbuilders amounted to 97.5 billion dollars in 2007, far exceeding the 31.3 billion dollars in 2005 and 61.7 billion dollars in 2006. In addition, locals rapidly increased foreign portfolio investments to 50.1 billion dollars in 2007, compared to 11.1 billion dollars and 24.1 billion dollars in 2005 and 2006,

31   See Ahn (2008), "Capital Flows and Effects on Financial Markets in Korea: Developments and Policy Responses," Financial Globalization and Emerging Market Capital Flows, BIS Papers No 44, September, pp. 307 and 317; and Yang and Lee (2008), "An Analysis of the Attractions of Arbitrage Transactions and of Domestic Bond Investment by Foreigners and Korean Branches of Foreign Banks (in Korean)," Monthly Bulletin, Bank of Korea, August. The article was written with the current author's assistance and comments.

Table 3.1 Amount of Shipbuilders' Order Books and Exchange Rate Hedging Ratios

(Billions of US dollars)

	2004	2005	2006	2007	2008	2009
FX forwards net selling (A)	12.50	16.82	35.25	53.26	41.67	16.07
Amount of order books (B)	31.80	31.27	61.70	97.50	71.79	18.33
Exchange rate hedging ratio (A/B, %)	39.3	53.8	57.1	54.6	58.0	87.6

Source : Park & Kwon (2010), "Effects on the Foreign Exchange Sector of Shipbuilders' Exchange Rate Hedging," Monthly Bulletin, Bank of Korea, February.

Table 3.2 Overseas Portfolio Investment[1] and Forwards Selling by Overseas Portfolio Investors[2]

(Billions of US dollars)

	2005	2006	2007	Jan.–Jun. 2008
Overseas portfolio investment	11.1	24.1	50.1	−1.1
(FX forwards net selling)	(1.5)	(13.1)	(27.2)	(3.7)

1. Based on "Foreign Exchange Supply and Demand Statistics."
2. Asset management companies, securities companies, etc.
Source : Yang & Lee (2008), "An Analysis of the Attractions of Arbitrage Transactions and of Domestic Bond Investment by Foreigners and Korean Branches of Foreign Banks (in Korean)," Monthly Bulletin, Bank of Korea, August.

respectively. In accordance with this, FX forwards selling by asset management companies surged.

As orders of shipbuilders and overseas portfolio investments by locals slowed remarkably in the wake of the global financial crisis in September 2008 and recent European fiscal crisis, the selling volume of their FX forwards for exchange rate risk hedging fell substantially. Reflecting this, the arbitrage incentive for three-year currency swaps decreased from 233 basis points in 2009 to 136 basis points in 2012, and that for the three-month FX swap also declined from 175 basis points to 51 basis points.

But current swap rate and CRS rate levels are still far above those of 2006 (19 basis points and 29 basis points, respectively), and thus a relatively high degree of arbitrage incentive persists. This is because export firms have tended to hedge foreign exchange risk through selling of FX forwards compared with import firms, as total exports exceed total imports. Export firms have also been much more sensitive to exchange rate risk than import firms. A further reason is because pressure for the sale of FX forwards still remains due to the rollover of existing forwards related to exchange rate risk hedging.

As described above, if the selling of FX forwards by export firms and asset management companies increases, commercial banks tend to expand their buying of FX forwards by the same amount. At the same time, commercial banks have to increase the sale of FX spot to balance their overall foreign exchange position, and raise foreign currency funds to sell from the swap market. This is why buy & sell swaps (or CRS receives) are structurally larger than sell & buy swaps (or CRS pays).

Some analysts endeavor to look for the cause underlying the imbalances in the swap market in the FX spot market. But I believe it is better to seek the cause in the FX forward market because it fundamentally arises from the FX forward market. For this reason, the introduction of a foreign exchange risk hedging ceiling on individual firms and an FX forward position limit on individual banks in 2010 is expected to bring about positive conditions conducive to a steady improvement in the imbalance in the FX forward market.

There is a second reason why substantial arbitrage incentives have persisted for so long. The sub-prime mortgage meltdown in the latter half of 2007, the global financial crisis of September 2008, and the escalation of the European fiscal crisis since the end of 2009 have made it difficult for foreigners to continue investing large funds into the local bond market. The following factors are thought to further increase this difficulty. Domestic bond investments by foreigners have already shown a substantial increase, while individual foreign investors tend to set a country investment limit on Korean bonds.

Because of the chronic oversold structure of the domestic FX forward market and difficulties in quickly resolving the European fiscal crisis, the swap market imbalances are expected to persist for a long time. Accordingly, arbitrage incentives will be maintained to a certain degree. If arbitrage incentives fall short of the expected level due to a lessening of the imbalances in the swap market, foreigners will take funds invested in the local bond market out. This will again restore the arbitrage incentives. In light of Korea's export and import structure and firms' exchange rate hedging practice, a certain degree of arbitrage incentives is likely to be maintained for a long time, and thus there is no option but to accept this situation. But if excessive imbalances in the swap market are left unattended for a long time, arbitrage incentives will continue to expand, resulting in negative effects such as the expansion of external debts through increased domestic bond investments by foreign bank branches and foreign investors.

In light of these points, it is better for the policy authorities to minimize excessive imbalances in the swap market than to aggressively seek a short-term fix. They should consistently strive to improve related systems to reduce imbalances in the FX forward market. In line with this, they should consider increasing the supply of foreign currency funds, if it is judged to be necessary, taking into account the degree of swap market imbalances and the volume of foreign exchange reserves. But they should keep in mind that the supply of foreign currency funds through the swap market would result in a reduction of foreign exchanges reserves.

On the other hand, some analysts argue strongly that it represents an outflow of national wealth for foreigners to take out substantial profits gained from investments in domestic bonds, by exploiting arbitrage incentives. But this claim seems to be misguided. Arbitrage incentives mainly come from structural factors in the domestic FX forward market, that is, the demand for exchange rate risk hedging by export firms. They set their export price, reflecting FX risk hedging costs. Foreigners take arbitrage profits by investing their funds in domestic bonds, while domestic firms get additional profits from exports. Therefore, it is difficult to characterize the

Figure 3.9 Flow Chart of Swap Market Imbalances

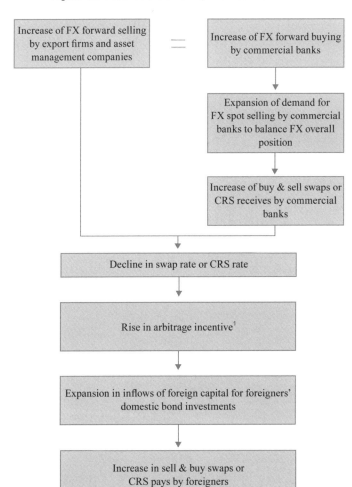

1. (Differential between domestic and international interest rates) – Swap rate
   = Yield on domestic bond – CRS rate

substantial arbitrage profits acquired from the domestic bond market by foreigners as an outflow of national wealth.

Improving the Swap Transaction Method

Another discussion point is the insistence that it is necessary for the Bank of Korea to improve the method of supplying foreign currency liquidity from swap market participation through agent banks to more market-oriented, competitive swap auctions. The insistence is thought to be valid in the sense that it can have the following positive effects.

First, the competitive swap auction method has an advantage that it may enhance the predictability and efficiency of the Bank's foreign currency liquidity supply. In October 2008, the Bank announced that the introduction of an auction method was aimed at attaining such goals. Second, this would contribute to eliminating misperceptions among market participants that the Bank's efforts are insufficient to ease swap market imbalances, despite the steady increase of foreign exchange reserves. So far, policy authorities have been understood to participate in the swap market from time to time, depending on foreign currency fund market conditions. Nevertheless, the concealment of the scale of their participation in the swap market may lead to the misunderstanding that they are not making adequate efforts, thus providing greater opportunities for arbitrage by foreign investors. In addition, the introduction of the auction method may help weaken the insistence of some market participants that the Bank should enhance the use of foreign exchange reserves. Third, the competitive swap auction method can bring about a signal effect through the disclosure of bidding amounts. This also helps the Bank gain information on the foreign currency funding situation of individual financial institutions and the overall swap market.

Therefore, it is desirable that current swap market participation method be changed to a purely competitive swap auction method in the near future. But until the swap market imbalances are substantially reduced, the Bank of Korea needs to employ the competitive swap auction method in tandem with the participation method.

chapter 4

Foreign
Exchange
Reserve
Management

Korea's foreign exchange reserves are assets held by the Bank of Korea and the government (Foreign Exchange Equalization Fund). But the management and operation of foreign exchange reserves are entrusted to the Bank of Korea.

When domestic financial institutions, corporations and individuals experienced a sharp depreciation of the won and severe recession during the 1977 currency crisis, an acute awareness arose the great importance of accumulating sufficient foreign exchange reserves. The foreign currency liquidity crisis in the wake of Lehman Brothers' collapse in September 2008 reconfirmed the importance of foreign exchange reserves.

This chapter first describes concept and function, operation and components, and changing factors of foreign exchange reserves. Then, it covers three important issues in Korea—excess or shortage of foreign exchange reserves, the conflict between safety and profitability, and the relationship between individual countries' foreign exchange reserves and the global financial safety net.

1. Concept of Foreign Exchange Reserves

Under the IMF guidelines, each member country reports statistics on foreign exchange reserves to the IMF on a monthly basis. According to the IMF's manual,[32] a country's "foreign exchange reserves"[33] are defined as "those external assets that are readily available to and controlled by the monetary authorities[34] for meeting balance of payments financing needs, for intervention in exchange markets to affect the currency exchange rate, and for other related purposes (such as maintaining confidence in the currency and the economy, and serving as a basis for foreign borrowing)." (BPM6, paragraph 6.64)

In accordance with this, foreign exchange reserves must have the following characteristics. First, foreign exchange reserves must be assets denominated in currencies widely and freely used internationally, such as the US dollar, the euro, the Japanese yen, or another international currency. Thus assets denominated in currencies that are not frequently used in

---

32   Sixth edition of the Balance of Payments and International Investment Position Manual (BPM6), August 2011.

33   "Foreign exchange reserves" are often referred to as "reserve assets," "official reserve assets," or "international reserves."

34   "Monetary authorities" is a functional concept that encompasses the central bank (which subsumes other institutional units, such as the currency board and certain operations usually attributed to the central bank but sometimes carried out by other government institutions or commercial banks, such as government-owned commercial banks. Such operations include the issuance of currency; maintenance and management of reserve assets, including those resulting from transactions with the IMF; and operation of exchange stabilization funds. (BPM6, paragraph 6.66)

international trade and financial transactions abroad cannot be included in foreign exchange reserves.

Second, foreign exchange reserves must be assets that are owned by monetary authorities and can be bought, sold, or liquidated for foreign currency (cash) at any time in the international financial markets. Therefore real estate, disqualified bonds with low credit ratings, and private funds are not included in foreign exchange reserves because they are not easily converted into foreign currency (cash). In addition, foreign currency assets that financial institutions and enterprises hold at home and abroad are not eligible as foreign exchange reserves.

Third, foreign exchange reserves must be foreign currency assets operated abroad by monetary authorities. Thus, foreign currency assets provided to domestic financial institutions and financial market through FX swaps and foreign currency loans are not classified as foreign exchange reserves.

According to this concept, Korea's foreign exchange reserves refer to external foreign currency assets owned by the Bank of Korea and the government (Foreign Exchange Equalization Fund). As foreign currency assets entrusted to the Korea Investment Corporation (KIC) by the Bank of Korea are invested only insofar as they maintain the characteristics of foreign exchange reserves under the Bank's investment guidelines, they are regarded as foreign exchange reserves.

2. Function of Foreign Exchange Reserves

A country's foreign exchange reserves are a nation's emergency funds that monetary authorities use as a last resort when a financial crisis erupts. In addition, they are used as an instrument to stabilize the external value (exchange rate) of the nation's currency, and play a role in maintaining or enhancing sovereign creditworthiness. Here is a closer look at the functions of foreign exchange reserves.

First, as we experienced during the currency crisis of December 1997 and foreign currency liquidity crisis of September 2008, massive foreign capital outflows, that is, foreign investors' abrupt withdrawals of their foreign currency loans and portfolio investment funds on a large scale from the domestic financial market, may be generated again in the future. In this event, if domestic financial institutions and enterprises cannot borrow foreign currency funds from abroad, and thus meet their obligations at maturity to foreign counterparties, then they will be seen as defaulting, and this may eventually bring about national insolvency. In such a case, if the central bank timely provides some part of the foreign exchange reserves to domestic financial institutions and market, such a crisis can be averted.

Second, in a country with a free-floating exchange rate system, significant volatility in exchange rates or one-sided transactions may occur in the foreign exchange market due to market participants' fears or speculative trading. When exchange rates move sharply due to temporary shortages of foreign currency, the policy authorities can release some part of the reserve assets to stabilize the foreign exchange market.

Third, holding sufficient foreign exchange reserves means that capacity for the settlement of payments is enough, helping to maintain or enhance the nation's creditworthiness. As such, international credit rating agencies take the volume of foreign exchange reserves as a key factor when assessing a country's sovereign credit rating. Even after Lehman Brothers' collapse in September 2008, Korea's sovereign credit rating remained at an investment grade of A3 (Moody's basis). Arguably, the sheer size of the country's volume of foreign exchange reserves (exceeding 200 billion US dollars at end-2008) played a large part in that outcome.

3. Components of Foreign Exchange Reserves

In general, central banks do not fully disclose detailed components of foreign exchange reserves. This is because the disclosure of specific information could cause large fluctuations in the international financial market by revealing a policy on the operation of foreign exchange reserves, such as changes in the composition of holding currencies and assets. Each member country reports basic data on its own reserve assets to the IMF on a monthly basis, and the IMF then publishes the data in its monthly International Financial Statistics (IFS), and on its website on international reserves and foreign currency liquidity.

In Korea, the Bank of Korea discloses the total volume and basic components of the holdings of reserve assets, based on the

Table 4.1 Composition of Korea's Foreign Exchange Reserves

(As of year-end, billions of US dollars)

	1997	2000	2005	2007	2008	2009	2010	2011	2012
FX reserves	20.4	96.2	210.4	262.2	201.2	270.0	291.6	306.4	327.0
Securities[1]	19.7[2]	90.6	186.8	231.8	180.4	248.9	267.9	277.9	299.9
Deposits	· ·	5.3	23.1	30.0	20.1	16.3	19.0	20.3	17.0
IMF Position	0.6	0.3	0.3	0.3	0.6	1.0	1.0	2.6	2.8
SDRs	0.06	0.0	0.04	0.07	0.09	3.7	3.5	3.5	3.5
Gold	0.04	0.07	0.07	0.07	0.07	0.08	0.08	2.2	3.8

1. Includes government bonds, government agency bonds, international financial institution (IFI)
   bonds, MBS, ABS, and others.
2. Includes deposits.
Source: Bank of Korea, Economic Statistics System (ECOS)

end of the previous month, at the beginning of every month. As of the end of 2012, Korea's foreign exchange reserves stood at 327.0 billion US dollars. In more specific terms, the country's foreign exchange holdings including securities and deposits stood at 316.9 billion dollars, 96.9 percent of total reserves, while its special drawing rights (SDRs) and IMF position totaled 3.5 billion dollars and 2.8 billion dollars, respectively. Korea's gold holdings were valued at 3.8 billion dollars, increasing 3.7 billion dollars in 2011 and 2012.

The Bank of Korea manages the nation's foreign exchange reserves to enhance profitability as well as to ensure liquidity and safety. To effectively accomplish these objectives, the Bank classifies the reserve assets into three categories by purpose: a liquidity tranche, an investment tranche, and an external management tranche, differentiating the operating purposes and methods by tranche. The liquidity tranche principally invests in short-term financial instruments such as US dollar-denominated short-term treasury bonds and deposits, thereby enabling a prompt response to regular frequent foreign exchange flows and to temporary demands for foreign exchange. In order to obtain stable profits, the Bank manages an investment tranche focusing on bonds denominated in the currencies of major developed countries, such as medium-and long-term government bonds, government agency bonds, corporate bonds and asset-backed securities. To acquire advanced investment techniques as well as to enhance profitability, the external management tranche is entrusted to internationally renowned asset management companies and the Korea Investment Corporation, and it is largely invested to bonds including mortgage-backed securities (MBS) and equities.[35]

The Bank of Korea has been publicizing information on the composition of reserve assets by purpose, currency and asset class on a yearly basis since 2007 to enhance the transparency of its management of reserve assets. Based on the composition of reserve assets as of the end of 2012, the investment tranche's share reached 79.4 percent, while the share of assets entrusted to external asset managers and that of the liquidity tranche stood at 16.7 percent and 3.9 percent, respectively. In terms of currency composition, assets were allocated among major currencies, including the US dollar, the euro, the Japanese yen and the British pound, to hedge the foreign exchange risk

35 See Annual Report of the Bank of Korea (2011), pp. 91–92.

of the reserves. As of the end of 2012, the share of US dollar denominated assets in the reserves reached 57.3 percent, while that of others showed 42.7 percent. This figure is slightly higher than the share of the US dollar in the world's total reserve assets (IMF basis), which stood at 61.2 percent. By asset class, the share of bonds issued by governments, government agencies and asset-backed securities reached 38.0 percent, 21.5 percent and 17.1 percent, respectively. In addition, the share of corporate bonds and stock holdings marked 12.9 percent and 5.7 percent, respectively.

Table 4.2 Percentage Shares of BOK's Foreign Currency Assets,[1] by Purpose, Currency, and Asset Class

(As of year-end, percent)

		2007	2008	2009	2010	2011	2012
By purpose	Liquidity tranche	3.9	5.8	1.9	3.2	4.5	3.9
	Investment tranche	84.5	76.1	84.0	82.5	79.7	79.4
	External management tranche	11.6	18.1	14.1	14.3	15.8	16.7
By currency	US dollars	64.6	64.5	63.1	63.7	60.5	57.3
	Others	35.4	35.5	36.9	36.3	39.5	42.7
By asset class	Deposits	7.4	8.4	4.0	6.0	6.6	4.8
	Securities						
	Government bonds	35.5	31.8	38.1	35.8	36.8	38.0
	Agency bonds	28.8	22.4	22.3	21.8	20.1	21.5
	Corporate bonds	15.4	16.9	15.1	16.5	14.1	12.9
	ABS	11.6	17.0	17.4	16.1	17.0	17.1
	Stocks	1.3	3.5	3.1	3.8	5.4	5.7
	Total	100.0	100.0	100.0	100.0	100.0	100.0

1. Represents the sum of securities and deposits in foreign exchange reserves in Table 4.1.
Source: Bank of Korea, Annual Report.

Comparison of Korea's Foreign Exchange Reserves with Those of Other Countries

As of the end of 2012, Korea's foreign exchange reserves reached 327.0 billion dollars, which were the seventh largest following China, Japan and Russia. In general, advanced countries do not have the need to accumulate large reserves because their sovereign creditworthiness is high and their currencies are widely used. But Japan's foreign exchange reserves are still the second largest in the world due to that country's efforts to ease the sharp appreciation of yen. Meanwhile, emerging economies tend to hold as large foreign exchange reserves as possible because the use of their currencies is limited in the international financial market, and because they also face difficulties in borrowing foreign currency funds during times of financial crisis.

Table 4.3 Major Countries' Foreign Exchange Reserves

(As of end-December 2012, billions of US dollars)

Rank	Country	FX reserves	Rank	Country	FX reserves
1	China	28,473	6	Brazil	2,916
2	Japan	10,962	7	Korea	2,886
3	Russia	4,794	8	Hong Kong	2,705
4	Switzerland	3,820	9	India[1]	2,687
5	Taiwan	2,973	10	Singapore	2,258

1. As of 28 December 2012.
Sources: IMF; websites of relevant central banks.

4. Factors behind Reserve Assets Changes

An assessment of foreign currency assets included in a country's foreign exchange reserves may be made at book value or market value. The Bank of Korea calculates its reserve assets based on the book value, and releases the data to the public at the beginning of every month. The amount of reserve assets varies, reflecting several factors, such as buying and selling of foreign exchange by the monetary authorities, profits gained from the investment of foreign currency assets, and fluctuations in exchange rates.

Korea has adopted a free-floating exchange rate system, but when the exchange rate shows rapid movements in the short term, policy authorities may intervene to buy or sell foreign exchange in the foreign exchange market in order to moderate the volatility. This is referred to as "smoothing operations." Buying foreign currency increases reserve assets, while selling foreign currency decreases them. The Korean government and the Bank of Korea do not announce the amounts of foreign currencies bought and sold.

The Bank of Korea gains profits including interest income from the investment of foreign currency assets. The profits themselves work as a factor in increasing reserve assets. The Bank invests its foreign exchange reserves in financial assets denominated in advanced countries' currencies such as the US dollar, the euro, the British pound, or the Japanese yen. The Bank of Korea translates other currency assets holdings into US dollar values in order to compile data on reserve assets and compare them with those of other countries. Accordingly, when

Table 4.4 Capital Outflows from Korea during Crises[1]

	Asian Currency Crisis (Nov. 1997–Mar. 1998)	Global Financial Crisis (Sep. 2008–Dec. 2008)
Total capital outflows	−21.4	−69.5
• Stock investment by foreign investors	2.1	−7.4
• Bond investment by foreign investors	−1.6	−13.4
• Short-term borrowings	−22.0	−48.7
Outstanding balance of short-term external debt[2]	. .	189.2

1. The crisis is defined as the period during which the capital account (based on BOP) recorded consecutive deficits.

2. Based on a remaining maturity basis, as of end-December 2008.

Source: Ministry of Strategy and Finance, Bank of Korea, etc. (2010), "New Macro-Prudential Measures to Mitigate Volatility of Capital Flows, Q&A," June 14.

other currencies appreciate against the US dollar, as the amount of other currency assets in US dollar terms increases, the volume of foreign exchange reserves expands. In contrast, when those currencies depreciate against the US dollar, as the amount of other currency assets translated into dollars decreases, the volume of the foreign exchange reserves shrinks.

5. Adequacy of Foreign Exchange Reserves

As part of securing a safety net for the country's economy, it is very important to hold more than the adequacy level of foreign exchange reserves. Some economists in academia and international financial organizations like the IMF and BIS have done research on the appropriate level of reserve assets. But, there has yet to be an internationally accepted standard for estimating the adequacy of a country's foreign exchange reserves. For instance, authoritative international financial organizations, and international credit rating agencies have yet to present an official metric for estimating an adequate level of foreign exchange reserves that can be universally applied to every country. This is because the degree of external dependency of an economy, the extent of capital liberalization, and various geopolitical risks are different from country to country. The demand for external payments in a country also varies frequently according to changing economic and financial conditions.

However, international credit rating agencies or commercial banks make frequent assessments of the level of a country's reserve assets, and these have a large impact on its sovereign credibility and on the overseas borrowings of its financial institutions as well as enterprises. For this reason, each country must hold a volume of reserve assets that does not fall short of meeting the demand for external payments when an emergency erupts, taking into account its particular economic and financial situation. In this respect, the policy authorities have to carefully look into the results of research conducted by international financial organizations and academia.[36] But it is not desirable

---

36　See, for example, BIS (2004), Flood & Marion (2002), Garcia & Soto (2004), Greenspan (1999), IMF (2011), Jeanne & Rancière (2005), and Wijnholds & Kapteyn (2001).

that a country's policy authorities should disclose the adequate amount or computation standard of its foreign exchange reserves because this is not only highly likely to have negative effects, but it may also bring about substantial difficulties in the conduct of foreign exchange policy.

In conclusion, Korea's foreign exchange reserves are foreign currency assets for external payments that are acquired in support of marketable liabilities (Treasury Bonds and Monetary Stabilization Bonds) issued by the government and the Bank of Korea in anticipation of an unexpected crisis. As the cost of holding foreign exchange reserves and the demand for external payments vary frequently according to changes in domestic and overseas conditions, it is not easy to judge whether the current volume of foreign exchange reserves is adequate or not. But Korea feels the necessity of holding a sufficient amount of foreign exchange reserves, considering its experiences with two previous crises and the Korean won's lack of internationalization. As Korea's foreign exchange reserves were almost completely depleted at the end of 1997, Korea was hit by a currency crisis, eventually receiving bailout funds from the IMF. However, at the time of the global financial crisis in September 2008, the nation maintained its foreign exchange reserves of more than 200 billion US dollars, helped by the expansion of reserve assets up to that time. As a result, even though experiencing foreign currency liquidity problem, Korea was able to overcome it relatively quickly.

6. Key Discussion Points

Three important issues hang over Korea's foreign exchange reserves. The first is related to the insistence on the adequacy of foreign exchange reserves. Second, some strongly advocate enhancing profitability, while others emphasize strengthening safety. The third issue is related to the argument that the establishment of global financial safety nets can replace an individual country's foreign exchange reserves or make up for a substantial portion of reserves.

Excess or Shortage of Foreign Exchange Reserves

Some economists insist that Korea's foreign exchange reserves must be expanded further to prepare for a future financial crisis. In contrast, other economists argue that part of the reserve assets should be used to assist domestic financial institutions and enterprises or for the development of overseas natural resources. This argument has lost ground since Korea experienced a severe foreign currency liquidity crisis as foreign banks and foreign investors withdrew massive amounts of both foreign currency loans and portfolio investment funds from the domestic financial market in the wake of Lehman Brothers' collapse in 2008. But if the volume of reserve assets continues to increase substantially over the coming years, this issue may resurface.

Given the lack of an international standard to judge whether a country's foreign exchange reserves are adequate or not, it becomes difficult to question the adequacy of current reserves. Moreover, even though any scholar or private research institution can put forward such an insistence, it is not appropriate for policy authorities or research institutions related to the government to take a position. If it is deemed that the volume of present reserve assets exceeds what is adequate, then it also means that policy authorities bought more foreign exchange than necessary. In other words, policy authorities overstepped their role in the foreign exchange market. Accordingly, if financial market participants understand that policy authorities do not need to buy additional foreign exchange in the foreseeable future, the exchange value of the Korean won is highly likely to depreciate sharply in the short term. Conversely, if the volume of current foreign exchange reserves is deemed less than adequate, the opposite results will occur.

Nevertheless, if some economists insist the volume of current reserve assets is inadequate, they should also present a resolution on how to secure the financial resources to buy foreign exchange to make up the shortfall. In Korea, the annual increase in the Foreign Exchange Equalization Fund needs the consent of the National Assembly. In addition, support from the Bank of Korea leads to monetary expansion, and additional issuance of Monetary Stabilization Bonds to absorb the extra liquidity brings about an increased burden on interest payments. Therefore, to expand foreign exchange reserves, the question of who will bear this cost must be also considered.

Some financial institutions and corporations argue that if policy authorities provide them with an excess portion beyond the adequate level of reserve assets at ordinary times, and then draw it down when necessary, this would not detract from the adequacy of the foreign exchange reserves. But the outbreak of a crisis makes it difficult for financial institutions and corporations to raise foreign currency liquidity overseas. At the time of Lehman Brothers' collapse, domestic financial institutions could not roll over even half of their maturing external liabilities due to the crisis. In the event of a shortage of foreign currency in the national economy, it would be difficult for domestic financial institutions and corporations to borrow new funds abroad. For this reason, it is virtually impossible for policy authorities to call in foreign currency funds provided to domestic financial institutions and corporations. In addition, in the event of the policy authorities providing reserve assets to specific enterprises, they should bear in mind that this may not only give rise to issues of equity at home but also incite a trade dispute, as it may be viewed as a form of subsidy payment prohibited under WTO agreements. Moreover, in the case of domestic financial institutions, if they were to rely on the central bank's supply of reserve assets without raising the necessary foreign funds on their own, this would negatively affect their credit rating and create moral hazard.

Taking into consideration all these points, I believe judging the adequacy of foreign exchange reserves should be assigned to the policy authorities. In light of the characteristics of foreign exchange reserves as a contingency fund, even if the level is more than necessary, it is desirable that an emerging market economy hold foreign exchange reserves as external assets with high safety and liquidity rather than long-term fixed assets during ordinary periods.

Necessity of Enhancing Safety or Profitability of Foreign Exchange Reserves

Some advocate that the Bank of Korea invest its foreign exchange reserves in foreign currency assets with high profitability even though the risk is higher compared with government bonds, to strike a balance between the costs and benefits of holding reserves. Other analysts argue that the Bank of Korea must further strengthen safety when investing reserve assets so that they can be mobilized when necessary, stressing that the insufficient use of reserve assets acted as a destabilizing factor in the domestic foreign exchange market during the global crisis.

In light of characteristics of the foreign exchange reserves, however, the investment of reserve assets should put priority on safety rather than on profitability. For this reason, the IMF does not classify foreign currency assets ineligible for investment grade as part of the foreign exchange reserves. In addition, it is a basic principle that a country's foreign exchange reserves must be invested in assets that can be readily liquidated for foreign currency (i.e., cash) at any time with minimum cost because they are not only foreign currency assets to be used during emergencies but they are also accompanied by liabilities. A country's reserve assets must be managed under principles different from those used by private financial institutions. It is not appropriate for policy authorities to invest reserve assets in the development of overseas natural resources or infrastructure projects because such investment funds are locked in for a long time and the risk related to collecting the principal is high.

Individual Country's Foreign Exchange Reserves and Global Financial Safety Net

After the Asian currency crisis in the late 1990's, many economists conducted empirical analyses on the relationship between the size of reserve assets and the probability of a crisis. Their research found that the more reserve assets, the lower the chances of a crisis, supporting the importance of sufficient accumulation of reserve assets. In fact, many emerging economies that experienced or faced a crisis expanded their reserve assets substantially as a prophylactic for crisis prevention. This is thought to have helped emerging economies sustain relatively stable growth without a severe crisis since the late 1990's.

However, Lehman Brothers' failure in September 2008 triggered an unprecedented crisis, not seen since the Great Depression of the 1930's. Under the strains of the global financial crisis, individual countries' efforts such as expansion of foreign exchange reserves proved to be limited. In response to this, the IMF introduced Flexible Credit Lines (FCL) in March 2009, giving drawing rights based on funds within ten times the quota for six months to one year to countries with favorable economic fundamentals and policies. In tandem with this, collective efforts to establish regional financial safety nets were increased. Typical of these were the Chiang Mai Initiative Multilateralization (CMIM) Agreement, the European Financial Stability Facility (EFSF), and the European Financial Stabilization Mechanism (EFSM).

The CMIM was launched on 24 March 2010 by creating a joint fund worth 120 billion US dollars with the objective to stabilize regional financial markets through the systematic assistance of US dollar liquidity. From the existing CMI bilateral swap network involving China, Japan and Korea and five ASEAN members, there emerged a stronger common decision-making mechanism under a single contract among ASEAN+3 member states and Hong Kong. CMIM provides financial support through currency swap transactions among CMIM participants when a crisis erupts. Each CMIM participant is entitled, in accordance with the procedures and conditions set out in the agreement, to swap its local currency against US dollars for an amount up to its contribution multiplied by its purchasing multiplier.

The EFSF and EFSM were established following decisions made on 9 May 2010 by the European Union (Ecofin) to prevent the fiscal crisis in Greece from spreading to neighboring countries. The EFSF was created as an interim organization or special purpose vehicle on 6 July 2010 by the euro member states. The EFSF's mandate is to safeguard financial stability in the eurozone by providing financial assistance to euro area members. To fulfill its mission, the EFSF issues bonds or other debt instruments in the capital markets. The EFSF is backed by guaranteed commitments from euro member states for a total of 780 billion euro and has lending resources of 440 billion euro. The EFSM was an emergency funding programme reliant upon funds raised in the financial markets and guaranteed by the European Commission using the European Union budget as collateral. It is run under the supervision of the Commission and aims to preserve financial stability in the European Union (EU) by providing financial assistance to eurozone member states. The Commission fund, backed by all 27 European Union members, has the authority to raise up to 60 billion euro. The EFSM has been in operation since 10 May 2010.

Despite the IMF's Flexible Credit Line (FCL) and regional financial safety nets, these mechanisms lacked sufficient financial resources in dealing with a global financial crisis. Accordingly, it was recognized that building global financial safety nets (GFSN) was necessary. The establishment of the GFSNs was proposed by the Korean government. After its adoption as a formal agenda item at the G20 Finance Ministry and Central Bank Governors meeting in Washington DC in April 2010, it was pursued with the goal of reaching agreement on them at the G20 Seoul Summit in November of that year.

At the G20 Seoul Summit, the Leaders all believed that "strengthened global safety nets can help countries to cope with financial volatility, reducing the economic disruption from sudden swings in capital flows and the perceived need for excessive reserve accumulation." For the next G20 summit, the Leaders asked their Financial Ministers and Central Bank Governors to prepare policy options to strengthen global financial safety nets.

In August 2010, the IMF revised its crisis prevention loan system as part of efforts to establish a global financial safety net.

First, the IMF enhanced the Flexible Credit Line (FCL), which was employed on a limited basis by only a very few countries, such as the extension of its duration to one to two years and the removal of the access cap. And as a new preventive tool, the IMF created a Precautionary Credit Line (PCL), allowing countries with sound fundamentals and policies, but not eligible for access to the FCL, to benefit from precautionary liquidity provisioning.

With regard to the establishment of global financial safety nets, the G20 has yet to lay out a specific detailed framework. But some progress has been made. For example, the IMF introduced the PCL and expanded the role of the FCL.

Meanwhile, regional financial safety nets in Asia and Europe have been strengthened. On 3 May 2012, the Finance Ministers and Central Bank Governors of ASEAN+3 committed to strengthening the CMIM as part of the regional financial safety net, and agreed to the following: (1) to double the total size of the CMIM from 120 billion US dollars to 240 billion US dollars; (2) to increase the IMF de-linked portion to 30 percent in 2012 with a view to increasing it to 40 percent in 2014 subject to review should conditions warrant.[37] And, the European Stability Mechanism (ESM) was formally inaugurated on 8 October 2012. The ESM has assumed the tasks fulfilled by the EFSF and the EFSM. The institutions will function concurrently until mid-2013, and the ESM will remain then

---

37 See "The Joint Statement of the 15th ASEAN+3 Finance Ministers and Central Bank Governors' Meeting (3 May 2012)."

as the sole and permanent mechanism for responding to new requests for financial assistance by euro area member states.

Efforts of major countries, international financial organizations, regional and G20 group countries to cope with the global financial crisis over the recent period provide some lessons for us. With globalization, many advanced and emerging economies have become intricately inter-connected through international trade and financial transactions. Accordingly, in case a financial crisis occurs in the future, it is highly likely to evolve into a regional or global crisis than be limited to a handful of countries. As the scale of a crisis widens and deepens, so do the costs for crisis prevention and resolution. Furthermore, it is difficult to predict in advance when, where, and what type of financial crisis may break out in the future. Therefore, it is important to strengthen joint response approaches at both regional and global levels with each country taking the responsibility of being sufficiently prepared.

At subsequent G20 Summits, establishing global financial safety nets will be the subject of active discussions, but progress on this matter will take time. For example, discussions over the establishment of a currency swap arrangement between advanced economies and emerging economies, which could be said to be the most effective global financial safety net, did not made much progress at the latest G20 Summit. Advanced economies such as the United States opposed it, citing the erosion of autonomy in their own monetary policies and the creation of moral hazard in emerging economies. The IMF's Precautionary Credit Line (currently Precautionary and Liquidity Line (PLL)) has been provided on a limited basis by only a very few countries, while regional financial safety nets established in Asia and Europe largely lack crisis prevention functions due to their linkage to the IMF's rescue fund.

In this situation, what should the policy authorities in Korea do to prepare against another financial crisis? First, they have to take an active role in the discussions regarding the establishment of global financial safety nets. In line with this, they ought also to strongly support that the CMIM system launched in March 2010 with other member states quickly takes deep root. Along with this, it will be necessary for them to actively propose a method to strengthen crisis prevention functions, such as the increase in the proportion delinked from the IMF's standby funds.

However, the present financial safety nets at the regional and global levels cannot replace Korea's own safety nets, and play mostly only a supplementary role. Accordingly, in order to cope with another financial crisis, Korea has no option but to strengthen its own safety nets. First, sound macroeconomic policies should be pursued. The policy authorities have to implement stable monetary policies and manage public finance prudently in order to ensure dangerous bubbles do not form in the national economy. Recently some European countries using the euro, the world's second reserve currency, have suffered recessions and massive unemployment due to excessive sovereign debt liabilities, eventually receiving rescue funds from the EU and the IMF. This experience should be a good lesson to us. And, regarding macroprudential soundness, the foreign exchange sector has been strengthened and reinforced much further than in the past, helped by the introduction of forward position limits, the setting of foreign exchange risk hedging limits on corporations, and the introduction of a macro-prudential stability levy. Such efforts need to be continued in the future.

The drive to ensure the adequacy of the foreign exchange reserves also needs to be constantly pursued. But, as the accumulation of reserve assets is accompanied by substantial costs such as the issuance of bonds, a comprehensive approach that includes elements such as the level of exchange rate, the volume of external debt, and the scale of foreigners' equity investments should be undertaken when the policy authorities increase foreign exchange reserves. In addition, the policy authorities must bear in mind that excessive accumulation of reserve assets should not invite the criticism that Korea profits through exchange rate manipulation. And, we should emphatically beware of calls for some of the reserve assets to be invested in the development of overseas natural resources.

In line with this, the Bank of Korea should endeavor to maintain close ties with major central banks including the US Federal Reserve. As we have found, currency swap arrangements between the Bank of Korea and the Federal Reserve played an important role in overcoming the country's foreign currency liquidity crisis during the global financial crisis.

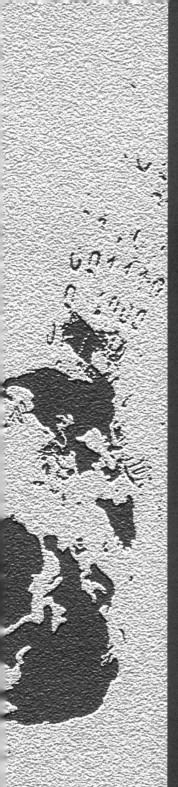

Chapter 5

External
Debt
Management

Korea's external debt statistics are published by the Bank of Korea on a quarterly basis. The volume and structure of external debt before and after Lehman Brothers' bankruptcy filing in September 2008 show remarkably different movements. From December 2005 to September 2008, gross external debt increased rapidly and the ratio of short-term debt to gross external debt jumped significantly. Subsequently, gross external debt decreased slightly until the end of December, 2010, since when it has gradually increased again. The weight of short-term debt in this has continued to decline at a fast pace.

This chapter describes the definition and classification of external debt by the IMF, and analyzes the reasons for the expansion of external debt before the collapse of Lehman Brothers, and its improvements since then. Lastly, issues regarding the appropriateness of the scale and structure of external debt, and currency and maturity mismatches in the banking sector are discussed.

1. Definition and Classification of External Debt

Definition of External Debt

According to the IMF manual,[38] gross external debt, at any given time, is defined as the outstanding amount of those actual current, not contingent, liabilities that require payments of principal and/or interest by the debtor at some point in the future and that are owed to nonresidents by residents of an economy. Accordingly, external debt statistics include only debt instruments, but exclude equity instruments. This is because equity means claims on the remaining value after all creditors have exercised claims; and thus it is not an actual current fixed liability.

Economic analysts at international financial organizations, credit rating agencies, and commercial banks, along with policy makers of both debtor countries and creditor countries make wide use of external debt statistics as basic data when evaluating the degree of external repayment burden and creditworthiness of a country. Debt statistics are also used to analyze various risks such as liquidity risk.

In order to enhance the usefulness of external debt statistics, it is above all important for each country to compile debt statistics that are comprehensive in coverage and have a

---

38   IMF (2003), "External Debt Statistics: Guide for Compilers and Users" (Final Draft, Nov. 2001), October.

high degree of comparability under globally uniform definitions and forms. For this reason, the IMF sought to create new guidelines, compiling external debt statistics jointly with the World Bank and other organizations. The guidelines, entitled, "External Debt Statistics: Guide for Compilers and Users," were released in November 2001. The IMF recommends that member countries compile and publish external debt statistics according to this guide.

Classification of External Debt, by Maturity, Sector, and Type

Most member countries of the IMF compile and publish external debt statistics by maturity, sector, and type, according to the guide. External debt by maturity is divided into short-term debt, defined as debt with a maturity of one year or less, and long-term debt, defined as debt with a maturity of more than one year, based on the formal criterion of original maturity at the time of borrowing. The outstanding amount and share of short-term external debt are widely used to detect liquidity risk. For more precise analysis of liquidity risk, it is necessary to look at all external debt due within a year. To do this, the IMF recommends member countries distinguish external debt with a remaining maturity of one year or less from long-term external debt. Generally, the figure summing up short-term external debt on an original maturity basis and long-term external debt due within one year is referred to as a short-term external debt on a remaining maturity basis. Despite its usefulness, most members of the IMF have not been compiling statistics on this due to difficulties in computation. Korea collected statistics for short-term external debt on a remaining maturity basis every quarter from end-December of 1997, but stopped in June 2009.

External debt is broken down by institutional sector, i.e., general government, monetary authorities, banks, and the other sectors. General government consists of central, state, and local governments, and all the social security funds operated at each of those levels. The monetary authorities sector is a functional concept in the balance of payments that covers the central bank and exchange stabilization funds of the government. The banking sector encompasses both commercial and savings banks. The other sectors comprise nonbank financial corporations, nonfinancial corporations, and household and nonprofit institutions. According to the characteristics of the financial instruments, external debt is classified into bonds, loans, trade credits, deposits, and others.

2. External Debt Developments

In January 2010, the IMF made a final draft of the sixth edition of the Balance of Payments and International Position Manual (BPM6), and recommended compliance by member states. In accordance with this, the Bank of Korea first changed its compilation method for current account and external debt data related to ship exports, and revised a series of historical data in December 2010. That is, the amount of ship exports counted at the time of delivery was changed to the time of installment payment received during ship building. In line with this, advances for ship exports that had been counted as an external debt in other sectors were excluded from external debt.

Expanding External Debt before the Collapse of Lehman Brothers

The volume and structure of external debt after Lehman Brothers' collapse in September 2008 showed significantly different movements, compared to those of the previous period. First, prior to Lehman Brothers' collapse, gross external debt as of the end of 2005 stood at 161.4 billion dollars, 5.9 billion dollars below the 167.3 billion dollars at end-1997. But it began to increase rapidly from 2006, registering a record high of 365.1 billion dollars at the end-September of 2009, the time of Lehman Brothers' collapse. It had accordingly expanded by 203.7 billion dollars in the two years and nine months since end-2005. In particular, short-term debt as of the end-September of 2008 had increased by 123.7 billion dollars compared to end-2005, and the ratio of short-term debt on an original maturity basis to gross external debt had risen sharply from 40.8 percent at end-2005 to 51.9 percent at the end-September of 2008. In addition, the ratio of short-term debt due within one year to gross external debt—frequently referred to as an indicator to evaluate the capacity of debt repayment—soared from 41.1 percent to 96.0 percent, near the critical value of stability level (100 percent), during the same period.

The rapid expansion of external debt, especially short-term debt, from 2006 to September 2008 was due to the following three factors. First, banks' short-term debt jumped due to an increase in FX forwards selling by shipbuilders and asset management companies. This actually led the expansion in gross external debt, pushing it up by 136.0 billion dollars, two-thirds of the overall increase in gross external debt (203.7 billion dollars) during this period. Banks bought the FX forwards that shipbuilders and asset management companies sold to hedge foreign exchange risk, and then they covered their over-bought position of FX forwards by selling FX spot with the use of short-term foreign currency borrowings. Domestic shipbuilders need to aggressively hedge exchange rate risk on advances received (about five installment payments) over an average three-year period as orders for ships unprecedentedly surged.

Meanwhile, the purchase of overseas funds by domestic individual investors expanded dramatically as the government gave incentives exempting them from taxes on capital gains generated from the investment of overseas funds. Most overseas funds at the time included commitments to hedge foreign exchange risk in the contract document, and so asset management companies conducted FX hedging. Hedging ratios at that time were estimated to be about 60 percent of total shipbuilding orders, and about 80 percent of overseas fund investments. Domestic banks that bought FX forwards from shipbuilders and asset management companies were forced to expand their short-term foreign currency borrowings from abroad, and at the same time, sell the funds in the FX spot market to balance the overall position of FX forward and spot.

Second, foreigners' investments in government bonds and monetary stabilization bonds expanded significantly. Along with this, external liabilities of general government and monetary authorities increased greatly, swelling by 15.6 billion dollars and 22.3 billion dollars, respectively, from January 2006 to September 2008. This was attributable to the fact that foreigners invested substantial funds in government bonds and monetary stabilization bonds as a result of the increase in the arbitrage margin in the domestic bond market triggered by subprime mortgage contagion in the second half of 2007. Foreigners' bond investments worked to increase external liabilities for the general government and monetary authorities, but they also eased instability in the swap market, and blunted the increase of external liabilities by banking sector as foreigners provided domestic banks with their funds through swap transactions for arbitrage gains.

Third, demand for foreign exchange linked with economic activity by export and import firms increased remarkably in tandem with rapid global economic growth. Trade financing and foreign currency loans increased by 19.4 billion dollars and 16.9 billion dollars, respectively, from January 2006 to September 2008. Such demand for foreign currency funds was included in the increment of external liabilities by the banking sector, as described above. During this period, external liabilities by other sectors increased by 29.8 billion dollars in line with expanded bond issuance and foreign currency borrowings from abroad by domestic firms.

Table 5.1 Trends of External Debt, by Sector, Maturity and Type

(As of period-end)

		1997	2005	2006	2007	Sep. 2008	2008	2009	2010	2011	2012
	Total external debt	167.28	161.41	225.20	333.43	365.09	317.37	345.68	359.76	398.72	413.44
Sector	General government	11.19	8.47	10.28	31.75	24.06	21.14	27.80	44.17	53.52	54.42
Sector	Monetary authorities	11.52	7.07	9.61	21.87	29.39	31.33	40.00	35.56	30.47	43.93
Sector	Depository institutions	91.05	83.43	136.54	192.88	219.45	169.42	180.26	173.08	196.34	183.83
Sector	Others	53.53	62.45	68.78	86.93	92.20	95.48	97.62	106.95	118.39	131.26
Maturity	Short-term	63.76	65.91	113.75	160.25	189.56	149.89	149.22	139.76	137.37	126.66
Maturity	(Short-term debt ratio)[1]	(38.1)	(40.8)	(50.5)	(48.1)	(51.9)	(47.2)	(43.2)	(38.8)	(34.5)	(30.6)
Maturity	Long-term	103.52	95.50	111.45	173.18	175.54	167.48	196.46	220.00	261.36	286.78
Type	Securities issuance	54.05	60.98	76.01	136.59	142.31	127.51	154.50	172.12	192.78	218.74
Type	Borrowings	104.84	75.64	122.84	162.91	186.96	140.98	145.45	135.31	145.79	131.41
Type	Cash and deposits	0.89	9.03	11.81	15.89	15.62	26.90	17.43	16.77	26.24	24.27
Type	Trade credits	6.36	6.74	7.49	8.27	9.25	9.80	11.86	17.27	14.81	15.53
Type	Others	1.14	9.03	7.06	9.77	10.97	12.18	16.44	18.28	19.12	23.49
	⟨reference⟩ Liquid External Debt[2]	86.33	86.41	134.06	203.99	229.97	189.23	··	··	··	··
	(Liquid External Debt Ratio)[3]	(973.0)	(41.1)	(56.1)	(77.8)	(96.0)	(94.0)	(··)	(··)	(··)	(··)
	FX reserves	8.87	210.39	238.96	262.22	239.67	201.22	269.99	291.57	306.40	326.97

1. External debt with one year or less of contractual maturity/Total external debt (%)
2. Means a short-term debt on a remaining maturity basis. It was only compiled until the end of March 2009.
3. Liquid external debt/Foreign exchange reserves (%).
Source: BOK, ECOS

External Debt Structure Improvements after the Collapse of Lehman Brothers

The upward trend of external debt stabilized rapidly, and its structure improved remarkably in the wake of the collapse of Lehman Brothers. Gross external debt as of end-2010 decreased to 359.8 billion dollars, 5.3 billion dollars less than that at end-September 2008. By sector, the government and monetary authorities' external liabilities increased by 26.3 billion dollars, while banks' external liabilities, which had led the increase in gross external debt before the demise of Lehman Brothers, shrank by 46.4 billion dollars. By maturity, long-term debt increased by 44.5 billion dollars, but short-term debt decreased by 49.8 billion dollars. As a result, the ratio of short-term debt to gross external debt dropped significantly from 51.9 percent at end-September 2008 to 38.8 percent by end-December 2010. The ratio of short-term debt on a remaining maturity basis to gross external debt also fell to 88.0 percent at end-March 2009. This was the last time the Bank of Korea disclosed this figure, but it is estimated to have declined further since.

The reduction of external debt and the improvement of its structure were helped by (1) rapid provision of foreign currency liquidity by policy authorities, (2) a favorable move of the foreign exchange situation due to a substantial current account surplus and large inflow of equity investment funds by foreigners, and (3) the introduction of FX forward position limits.

First, let us review policy measures that provided banks with foreign currency liquidity. Immediately after Lehman Brothers' collapse in September 2008, domestic banks faced a severe shortage of foreign currency liquidity owing to deleveraging by foreign bank branches and foreigners, leading to severe destabilization of the foreign exchange and swap markets. To ease this situation, the Ministry of Strategy and Finance supplied around 30 billion dollars through swap transactions, competitive bidding for foreign currency loans, and export and import refinancing.

The Bank of Korea also provided banks with 26.8 billion dollars through competitive swap auctions and foreign currency loans by using the official foreign exchange reserves and the dollar proceeds of swap transactions with the Federal Reserve

Table 5.2 Provision and Withdrawal of FX Liquidity by Korean Government and Bank of Korea following Lehman Brothers' Collapse

(Billions of US dollars)

Type		FX Liquidity Provision		Final Withdrawal
		Amount	Period	
MOSF[1] (30.03)	Swap transactions	10.00	Oct.–Dec. 2008	Nov. 2009
	Competitive auction loan	9.20	Nov. 2008–Jan. 2009	Jun. 2009
	Export-import finance support	10.83	Nov. 2008–Feb. 2009	Dec. 2009
Bank of Korea (26.77)	Competitive auction swap	10.27	Oct.–Dec. 2008	Aug. 2009
	Competitive auction loan under Fed currency swap	16.35	Dec. 2008–Jan. 2009	Dec. 2009
	Loans secured by export bills	0.15	Dec. 2008–Feb. 2009	Jul. 2009
Total		56.80		

1. Figures estimated by government.

Sources: Ministry of Strategy and Finance (MOSF); Bank of Korea

between October 2008 and February 2009. As banks repaid substantial amounts of foreign currency borrowings with the foreign currency funds that the government and the Bank of Korea supplied, external liabilities by the banking sector were reduced by 50 billion dollars during the fourth quarter of 2008.

In addition, the remarkable improvement of the external debt structure after 2009 could be realized, thanks to a favorable turn in supply and demand conditions for foreign exchange. This was mainly attributable to a substantial surplus on the current account and large inflows of foreigners' equity investments. The current account surplus stood at 3.2 billion dollars in 2008, but expanded rapidly to 32.8 billion dollars by 2009, a record high since 1999, that was followed by 28.2 billion dollars in 2010. Combined with improvements in other macroeconomic indicators, all this provided momentum to create for Korea a reputation of having a capacity for economic resiliency far exceeding most other countries. Whether the surplus trend of current account would continue or not was recognized to be a main criterion in judging the country's international competitiveness and capacity for external debt repayment. As domestic portfolio investments by foreigners were active, based on such recognition, the total amount of inflows of equity investment funds during 2009 and 2010 registered 48.6 billion dollars, far exceeding the amount of outflows at the time of the global crisis (33.5 billion dollars in 2008). In addition, domestic bond investments by foreigners increased rapidly from 4.0 billion dollars in 2008 to a total of 29.5 billion dollars in 2009 − 2010.

Meanwhile, the favorable turn in foreign currency liquidity

conditions allowed the government and the Bank of Korea to withdraw all foreign currency funds provided when the crisis was at its peak in a gradual and flexible manner between March and December of 2009. Thanks to these efforts, the nation's foreign exchange reserves expanded greatly from 201.2 billion dollars at the end of 2008 to 270.0 billion dollars at the end of 2009, and to 291.6 billion dollars at end-2010. In line with a steady increase in external assets, net external assets reached 91.3 billion dollars as of end-2010, three times more than the 24.6 billion dollars at end-2008. The collection of these foreign currency funds by the policy authorities was positive in that domestic banks raised foreign currencies by themselves,

Table 5.3 Trends of Current Account, Foreign Investor Stock Investment and External Claims Balance

(Billions of US dollars)

	1997	2005	2006	2007	2008	Jan.-Sep. 2008	2009	2010	2011	2012
Current account[1]	−8.18	18.61	14.08	21.77	3.20	−3.30	32.79	29.39	26.07	43.25
Foreigners' stock investment[1]	0.78	−1.39	−13.27	−28.94	−33.47	−29.28	25.07	23.55	−7.60	16.91
Net external claims (B-A)[2]	−61.13	155.66	155.70	83.65	24.55	30.60	69.00	91.30	97.96	122.46
External debts (A)[2]	167.28	161.41	225.20	333.43	317.37	365.09	345.68	359.76	398.72	413.44
External claims (B)[2]	106.15	317.07	380.90	417.08	341.92	395.69	414.68	451.06	496.69	535.90
FX reserves[2]	8.87	210.39	238.96	262.22	239.67	201.22	269.99	291.57	306.40	326.97

1. Based on BOP; Figures of '+' or '−' represent net inflows or net outflows during period, respectively.
2. Based on outstanding balance at period-end.
Source: BOK, ECOS.

nurturing their capacity to manage liquidity risk more effectively. It was thought to be in part a result of these efforts that, on 2 September 2009, Fitch Ratings upgraded Korea's sovereign credit rating of A+ from negative outlook to stable outlook, which was the level prior to the crisis.

In 2010, the government and the Bank of Korea took the requisite measures, analyzing various alternatives to moderate major fluctuations in capital inflows and outflows, based on their experiences from the global financial crisis. Typical among them was a forward position limit system introduced on July 9, 2010 (effective from October 9). The system was a macroprudential measure to prevent the sudden surges in foreign capital from increasing the instability of foreign exchange and foreign currency fund markets. In the boom of 2006 and 2007, banks had bought an excessive volume of FX derivatives including forwards from export firms, substantially expanding their external liabilities (mainly short-term debt). But this risk subsided significantly in the wake of the crisis. This new system helped to sooth short-term market shocks, thanks to thorough preparation and advance notification. Short-term external debt in the banking sector decreased by 14.8 billion dollars in the second half of 2010 when the system was introduced, in sharp contrast to the first half of 2010 (an increase of 1.2 billion dollars).

Meanwhile, the Financial Services Commission and the Financial Supervisory Service unveiled the "Plan for Financial Institutions' FX and Soundness & Strengthened Supervision" in November 2009, in response to financial institutions' foreign exchange weaknesses brought to light during the crisis. In accordance with this plan, measures were taken to improve the current system, such as tightening of regulation regarding the ratio of long-term foreign currency financing for foreign currency loans, and the establishment of new risk management standards for FX derivatives trading. These efforts also contributed to the improvements in external debt structure such as the reduction of short-term debt and the drop in its ratio to total debt in 2010.

However, gross external debt increased again gradually from 2011 due to continued inflows of foreigners' bond investment funds and the issuance of bonds abroad by public corporations to raise funds for the development of overseas natural resources. Gross external debt registered 413.4 billion dollars at end-2012, increasing by a total of 53.7 billion dollars in 2011−2012. The ratio of short-term debt to gross external debt, however, dropped from 38.8 percent at the end of 2010 to 30.6 percent at the end of 2012, helped by the decrease in the short-term debt of foreign bank branches and the expansion of medium-and long-term funding of domestic banks.

3. Key Discussion Points

Two main discussion points should be raised regarding Korea's external debt. One is whether the volume and structure of external debt at present are appropriate or not. The other is whether or not currency and maturity mismatches in the banking sector will create financial system risk.

Appropriateness of External Debt

It is not easy to judge whether the level of external debt in a country is appropriate or not. This is because there is no universal criterion available. In general, indicators presented in the "Report of Global Development Finance" by the World Bank are cited frequently to evaluate the volume and structure of external debt. They are elaborated to evaluate external debt of developing countries facing difficulties with external payments, and are divided into solvency and liquidity indicators. Solvency indicators include a ratio of external debt to nominal gross national income (GNI), a ratio of external debt to current receipts, and a debt service ratio (DSR). Liquidity indicators include a ratio of short-term debt on an original maturity basis to total external debt, and a ratio of external debt maturing within one year to GDP. The IMF and international credit rating companies use similar indicators to evaluate external debt of a country as a whole, even though there is a small difference in the scope of each item. But the World Bank sets a significance level for each indicator, and often revises the significance levels of some indicators in line with conditions when necessary.

It is hard to use these indicators as general criteria to evaluate the situation of external debt of individual countries. Why is that? First of all, it is meaningless to compare absolute levels of external indicators because the level of income, market openness and degree of market development, and exchange rate system differ from country to country. For example, the volume of external debt and the ratio of short-term debt of most advanced countries tend to be larger, compared with those of developing countries. This is because foreign investors prefer buying bonds issued by governments and corporations of advanced countries, considering their high creditworthiness and international competitiveness as well as the degree of openness and development of financial markets. In addition, it is because banks and enterprises of advanced countries can make foreign currency borrowings and financial derivatives transactions, based on their high credit rating.

Therefore, indicators to evaluate external debt and their critical values presented by the World Bank should be used to compare external debt among developing and low-income countries. It does not seem to be valid to judge the status of external debt by applying the same indicators to the advanced countries. The IMF and World Bank believe that simple comparisons of indicators to evaluate external debt among countries are meaningless, and critical values of individual indicators are not absolute criteria. In addition, they classify into advanced economies (high-income countries) and developing countries (low-income countries) based on the stage of economic development and the level of national income, excluding the former from countries that should report to the "Debtor Reporting System." Korea was also classified as an advanced economy by the IMF and World Bank in 1997 and 2003, respectively, and excluded from countries that should report to the "Debtor Reporting System."[39] In fact, main debt

---

39　IMF (1997), World Economic Outlook (Statistical Appendix), May.

Table 5.4 World Bank External Debt Assessment Indicators[1]

(Percent)

Solvency indicators	High-debt countries	Mid-debt countries	Low-debt countries	Korea						
				1997	2000	2005	2008	2009	2010	2012
• External debt/Nominal GNI[2]	above 80 (above 50)	48–80 (30–50)	less than 48 (less than 30)	31.6	26.6	19.1	33.8	41.2	35.4	36.4
• External debt/Current revenue[3]	above 220	132–220	less than 132	101.1	67.5	47.5	60.4	80.1	65.6	62.3
• DSR[4]	above 30	18–30	less than 18	12.4	14.7	10.2	7.7	10.4	10.3	8.8
Liquidity indicators	risky	vigilant	stable							
• Liquid external debt ratio[5]	above 200	100–200	less than 100	973.0	73.2	41.1	94.0	··	··	··
• Short-term external debt ratio[6]	critcal if above 60		less than 60	38.1	35.1	40.8	47.2	43.2	38.8	30.6

1. Based on "2010 Balance of Payments and International Investment Position Manual."
2. Figures in ( ) represent critical ranges before 2003.
3. Current Revenue = Goods exports + Service revenue.
4. Debt Service Ratio = (Long-term external debt principal + Long-and short-term external debt interest payments)/Current revenue
5. Liquid external debt (External debt with one year or less of remaining maturity)/Foreign reserves; but liquid external debt was only compiled until the end of March 2009.
6. Short-term external debt (External debt with one year or less of contractual maturity)/Total external debt
Sources: World Bank (2002), Global Development Finance; BIS, IMF, OECD & World Bank, Joint BIS-IMF-OECD-World Bank Statistics on External Debt (2001), November.

burden indicators in Korea showed stable movements below critical values of less indebted countries from the start of 2000.

Second, the potential capacity to service the debt and the structure of external debt in a country changes frequently according to domestic and international conditions. In particular, evaluating a country's debt servicing capacity should take into account various factors including official foreign exchange reserves, the structure of assets and liabilities of commercial banks and their capacity to repay their debt by themselves, the current account position, and conditions for raising foreign currency, not to mention the volume and structure of external debt. Thus, even though external debt may be deemed to be appropriate at a specified time, the appropriateness of external debt in a country should be carefully analyzed, taking changing conditions into consideration, as its debt servicing capacity changes with macroeconomic indicators. The IMF also recommends investigating the changing trend of debt indicators in the medium term, comprehensively considering the conditions of economic fundamentals including the current account and exchange rate system.[40]

Third, it is not easy to explain the gap between quantitative evaluation based on these criteria and the perceptions as to appropriateness in the international financial market at the start of the financial crisis. Actually, at the time of the global financial crisis in 2008, Korea was in a favorable situation among advanced economies based on key debt burden indicators presented by the World Bank as well as macroeconomic indicators including economic volume and income level. Nevertheless, Korea was considered to be one

---

40   IMF (2003), External Debt Statistics: Guide for Compilers and Users (Final Draft, Nov. 2001), October, pp. 171–176.

of the weaker countries in regard to debt servicing capacity by the foreign media. From early July of 2008—in the run-up to Lehman Brothers' collapse—doubts about Korea's debt servicing capacity emerged in international financial markets, compared with emerging economies and low-income countries whose economic power and external creditworthiness were far below those of Korea.

As soon as Lehman Brothers filed for bankruptcy in mid-September of 2008, foreigners withdrew funds on a massive scale, and domestic commercial banks faced difficulties in rolling over maturing foreign currency loans as well as in borrowing new foreign funds. Subsequently, Korea faced a severe shortage of foreign currency liquidity.[41] This was because Korea was recognized as a hybrid, strong economically and institutionally like an advanced economy, but weak like an emerging economy due to its high dependency on trade as well as overseas capital and finance. Foreigners have tended to expand portfolio investment during boom periods, based on the country's high degree of openness and favorable macroeconomic indicators, but withdraw foreign capital rapidly in downturns or with signs of a crisis. Such high external dependency has been inevitable for a small open economy, like Korea's.

The current volume and structure of external debt in

---

41   The refinancing ratio of domestic banks' short-term overseas borrowings fell to 39.9 percent in October 2008 from 99.8 percent during the third quarter of 2008. Refer to "Domestic Banks' Long-term Funding Resources as of end-May 2009," Financial Supervisory Service, 1 July 2009.

Korea are more stable than in September 2008 when Lehman Brothers collapsed. But should financial and economic conditions significantly deteriorate, it is difficult to say whether Korea's external debt position will remain calm in the future. Despite Korea's steady economic development, the country is still recognized as a small open country with a high degree of external dependency, high geopolitical risk, and carrying for the stigma of previous currency crises.

In fact, Korea's ratio of exports and imports to GDP is one of the highest in the world, while its ratio of external debt to GDP is far lower than those of advanced economies, but higher than those of other emerging economies such as Brazil, Russia,

Figure 5.1 Selected Countries' Degree of Trade Dependence in 2011

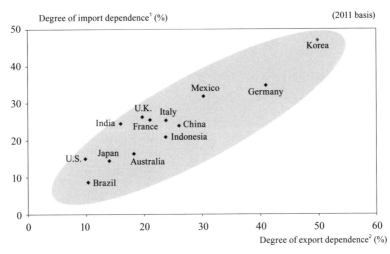

1. Imports (C.I.F)/GDP.
2. Exports (F.O.B)/GDP.
Source: IMF, Principal Global Indicators.

India, and Mexico (with lower credit ratings than Korea's). This shortcoming may actually be a cause of negative evaluations of Korea's debt servicing capacity by international financial market when a crisis occurs.

Therefore, even though current external debt is stable in light of quantitative indicators, the government should carry out the thoroughgoing management of external debt in normal times to prevent its excessive expansion and structural deterioration in the years ahead. Along with this, it should continue to foster crisis response capacity by further lowering Korea's dependency on external debt and adopting additional

Figure 5.2 Selected Countries' Credit Ratings and Degree of Dependence on External Debt in 2011

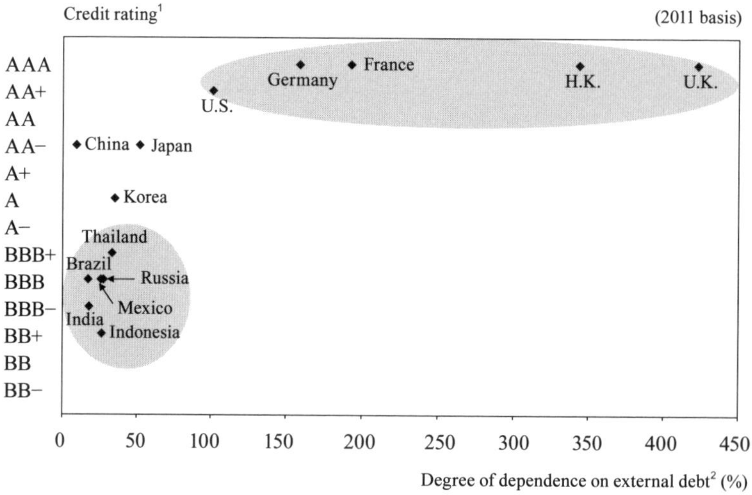

1. Based on Standard & Poor's Rating.
2. External Debt/GDP.
Sources: IMF; Bloomberg; Standard & Poor's Ratings Services; BOK, ECOS.

prudential measures that limit excessive demand for foreign currency funds.

Currency and Maturity Mismatches in the Banking Sector

Some economists maintain that because the size of currency and maturity mismatches between foreign currency assets and liabilities in the banking sector is large, the chances of systemic risk are high when domestic and external shocks occur. The size of currency mismatches can be measured as the difference between external foreign currency assets and liabilities. The size of the maturity mismatch in the banking sector is also calculated as the difference between external foreign currency assets and liabilities by maturity (i.e., short term and long term). The banking sector has faced chronic currency mismatches because external foreign currency liabilities have always exceeded external foreign currency assets. As short-term external foreign currency liabilities have been very heavy, the size of short-term maturity mismatches has been larger than that of long-term maturity mismatches.

This is because domestic banks have no option but to borrow foreign currencies abroad to provide firms with the necessary funds, while foreign bank branches borrow foreign currency funds abroad (mostly from their head offices) to conduct local business and investment on domestic bonds. The size of the currency mismatch of banking sector stood at 30.4 billion dollars at the end of 2005, but jumped to 134.5 billion dollars at end-September 2008. During the same period, the maturity mismatch surged from 12.3 billion dollars to 106.4 billion dollars. Foreign bank branches, in particular, provided domestic banks with a large amount of short-term foreign currency borrowings through sell & buy swaps in the wake of the rapid expansion of forward exchange selling by exporters. Accordingly, the size of currency and maturity mismatches increased immensely.

Because of wholesale deleveraging by foreign bank branches and foreigners due to Lehman Brothers' collapse in September 2008, such large currency mismatches led to a severe shortage of foreign currency liquidity among domestic banks. But thanks to the rapid provision of foreign currency

Figure 5.3 Size of External Currency Mismatch[1] of Banks (quarterly), 2005–2012

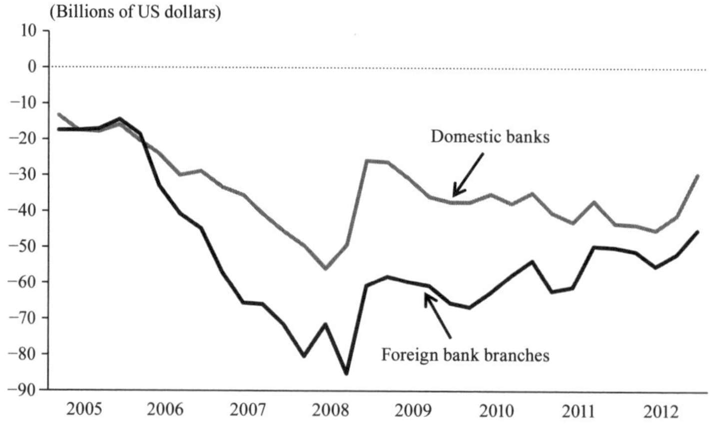

1. External foreign currency asset − External foreign currency liability on B/S of domestic banks and foreign bank branches in Korea.
Source: BOK, ECOS.

Figure 5.4 Size of External Maturity Mismatch[1] of Banks (quarterly), 2005-2012

Domestic Banks

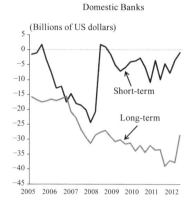

Foreign Bank Branches

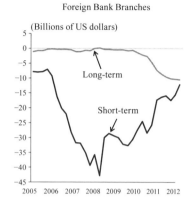

1. Short-term (long-term) external foreign currency assets – short-term (long-term) external foreign currency liabilities of domestic banks in Korea.
   Source: BOK, ECOS.

1. Short-term (long-term) external foreign currency assets – Short-term (long-term) external foreign currency liabilities of foreign bank branches in Korea.
   Source: BOK, ECOS.

liquidity by the government and the Bank of Korea, external debt in the banking sector decreased substantially. As a result, the size of currency and short-term maturity mismatches narrowed significantly to 88.3 billion dollars and 52.0 billion dollars, respectively, as of the end of 2010. They improved further, declining to 74.5 billion dollars and 25.2 billion dollars, respectively, as of the end of 2012.

Meanwhile, the net external assets of monetary authorities amounted to 288.7 billion dollars as of end-December 2012. This was about 214 billion dollars larger than the banking sector's currency mismatch, and about 264 billion dollars bigger than the short-term maturity mismatch. We can say this

Table 5.5 Trends of External Debts and Claims in Banking Sector, by Maturity

(As of period-end, billions of US dollars)

		2005	2006	2007	Sep. 2008	2008	2009	2010	2011	2012
Banking sector external debts (A)		83.4	136.5	192.9	219.5	169.4	180.3	173.1	196.3	183.8
Long -term	Domestic banks	30.4	37.9	54.3	56.6	54.4	59.3	62.1	71.0	71.8
	Foreign bank branches	1.7	2.6	4.6	3.5	4.6	5.3	8.9	22.3	26.3
Short -term	Domestic banks	28.0	44.3	54.6	65.5	42.6	43.7	43.8	58.7	49.7
	Foreign bank branches	23.3	51.8	79.4	93.9	67.8	72.0	58.3	44.3	36.1
Banking sector external claims (B)		53.0	63.2	76.4	85.0	82.7	77.6	84.8	103.3	109.4
Long -term	Domestic banks	12.9	21.4	27.6	28.1	26.7	29.2	30.2	37.6	43.3
	Foreign bank branches	1.1	1.9	3.3	3.9	4.0	4.3	4.5	5.4	5.5
Short -term	Domestic banks	29.7	32.0	36.1	44.7	44.4	36.6	41.0	48.8	48.9
	Foreign bank branches	9.4	7.9	9.4	8.3	7.7	7.5	9.1	11.5	11.7
Banking sector net external claims (B−A)		−30.4	−73.4	−116.5	−134.5	−86.7	−102.6	−88.3	−93.1	−74.5
Long -term	Domestic banks	−17.5	−16.5	−26.8	−28.6	−27.7	−30.1	−32.0	−33.4	−28.5
	Foreign bank branches	−0.6	−0.7	−1.3	0.4	−0.7	−1.0	−4.3	−17.0	−20.7
Short -term	Domestic banks	1.7	−12.3	−18.6	−20.8	1.8	−7.1	−2.8	−10.0	−0.9
	Foreign bank branches	−14.0	−43.9	−69.9	−85.6	−60.2	−64.5	−49.2	−32.7	−24.3

Source: BOK, ECOS.

Table 5.6 Trends of External Debts and Claims, by Sector

(As of period-end, billions of US dollars)

	2005	2006	2007	Sep. 2008	2008	2009	2010	2011	2012
External debt (A)	161.41	225.20	333.43	365.09	317.37	345.68	359.76	398.72	413.44
(Monetary authorities)	7.07	9.61	21.87	29.39	31.33	40.00	35.56	30.47	43.93
(Depository institutions)	83.43	136.54	192.88	219.45	169.42	180.26	173.08	196.34	183.83
External claims (B)	317.07	380.90	417.08	395.69	341.92	414.68	451.06	496.69	535.90
(Monetary authorities)	213.44	243.94	267.46	244.46	205.58	275.12	296.23	311.10	332.56
(Depository institutions)	53.04	63.16	76.37	84.95	82.70	77.64	84.77	103.25	109.37
Net external claims (B–A)	155.66	155.70	83.65	30.60	24.55	69.00	91.30	97.96	122.46
(Monetary authorities)	206.37	234.33	245.59	215.08	174.25	235.12	260.67	280.63	288.64
(Depository institutions)	−30.39	−73.37	−116.51	−134.50	−86.72	−102.63	−88.31	−93.09	−74.47

Source: BOK, ECOS.

implies that the monetary authorities have enough capacity to provide the banking sector with foreign currency liquidity, in case it faces a crisis of foreign currency liquidity. In this respect, even though domestic and external shocks may occur in the near future, the probability of current currency and maturity mismatches posing increased risks to the financial system is not considered large.

Quantitative analysis alone, however, cannot provide complete security regarding currency and maturity mismatches in the banking sector. Even if the volume of official foreign exchange reserves is large enough, a continuous decrease in the reserves will be a key factor in lessening the creditworthiness of the government, making it difficult to perform the function as lender of last resort over a long period. In addition, we must remember that if domestic banks continue their overreliance on foreign currency liquidity via monetary authorities, their credit ratings will be downgraded, eventually negatively affecting the country's sovereign rating.[42]

Therefore, to lesson chronic currency and maturity mismatches in the banking sector, the government should strengthen banking supervision, limiting the excessive increase of FX derivatives, such as FX forwards buying, as well as the raising of foreign currency funds with short-term maturities. In line with this, the government should steadily reinforce prudential measures, such as FX forward position ceilings. Furthermore, in the medium and long term I think it is necessary to consider proposals for extending the current application of the foreign currency liquidity ratio to domestic banks to cover foreign bank branches as well.

42 On 10 November 2008, Fitch Ratings lowered credit ratings on major domestic banks, considering that official foreign exchange reserves were feared to decline owing to the monetary authorities' supply of foreign currency liquidity to them, and their increased dependency on the monetary authorities. Fitch Ratings also downwardly adjusted the nation's sovereign credit rating of A+ from stable outlook to negative outlook.

Chapter 6

Capital
Liberalization

Full-scale capital liberalization in Korea was undertaken in the wake of its entry into the OECD in December 1996 and the currency crisis at end-1997. In particular, in April 1999, the government comprehensively revised the legal framework for foreign exchange and capital transactions from the Foreign Exchange Management Act established in 1962 to the Foreign Exchange Transactions Act. Along with this, the method of regulating capital transactions shifted from a 'positive system,' one that in principle controls them but liberalizes them only in exceptional cases, to a 'negative system,' under which in principle all foreign exchange transactions are permitted and only specific transactions are prohibited. With nearly all capital transactions liberalized, the degree of Korea's capital market liberalization is now considered to be on a par with advanced countries.

This chapter explains the meaning and effects of capital liberalization, and then describes the process of capital liberalization in Korea, focusing on domestic securities investments by nonresidents as well as overseas securities investments by residents, which both have a large impact on the domestic financial and foreign exchange markets. Lastly, several ways to respond to excessive capital inflows and outflows are discussed.

1. Meaning and Effect of Capital Liberalization

Capital liberalization in a country refers to the free movement of foreign currencies and its own currency in capital transactions between residents and nonresidents, as distinct from current transactions such as exports/imports of goods and services. This book covers only the liberalization of foreign capital movements, and does not deal with the liberalization of the country's local currency, that is, its internationalization. In emerging market economies generally, the internationalization of the local currency has not been achieved to any great degree.

Capital liberalization has both positive and negative effects on a nation's economy. One positive aspect is the ability of countries facing a shortage of domestic capital and natural resources to raise the foreign capital necessary for economic development. It also makes it possible for financial institutions and corporations to acquire the foreign capital necessary for loans and imports, respectively, at a lower cost (interest rate) than to raise domestic funds. In addition, it helps to facilitate the development of domestic financial and foreign exchange markets. However, substantial and persistent inflows of foreign capital may cause the expansion of the money supply, the rapid decline of exchange rates (currency appreciation), and asset price bubbles. In contrast, massive outflows of foreign capital in a short period may bring about financial market instability, such as a steep drop in equity prices and sharp depreciation of the local currency. In addition, it may result in the failure of financial institutions whose foreign exchange liquidity management is weak, and furthermore may trigger the collapse of the country's foreign exchange and financial systems.

Because of these two aspects of capital liberalization, emerging market economies have implemented capital liberalization gradually, in consideration of their stage of economic development, and degree of financial market development. But advanced countries have almost completely opened their capital markets. Generally, capital liberalization is first directed to domestic investments by nonresidents, and then overseas investments by residents, while domestic investments by nonresidents first target direct investments, and then portfolio investments.

Process of Capital Liberalization in Korea

Capital liberalization in Korea began by allowing direct investments by foreigners with the establishment of the Foreign Capital Introduction Facilitation Act, which stipulated the provision of tax exemption benefits, and guarantees of principal withdrawal and profits remittance in January 1960. But foreigners' direct investment was not active until the end of 1970s due to its negative perception such as foreigners' control of domestic industries and deepening dependency on foreign capital.

From the start of the 1980s, capital liberalization expanded in line with a policy of opening. Foreigners' portfolio investment was achieved by indirect methods, such as the permission of beneficiary stocks issuance by investment trust companies in October 1981 and the allowance of the purchase/

sale of domestic stocks by foreigner exclusive investment companies in June 1984. From July 1984, the scope of business to allow foreigner direct investment was expanded. By 1992, the equity market was partially opened to foreigners, and then capital liberalization was implemented on a full scale in the wake of the country's entry into the OECD in December 1996 and the currency crisis at end-1997. In particular, following the Asian financial crisis, the expansion of foreign exchange reserves became a top national priority, thus increasing the need to attract foreign capital. In accordance with this, the Korean government began liberalizing foreigner direct and indirect investments completely by abolishing ceilings on bond and equity investments by end-1997 and May 1998, respectively, and by shifting foreigner direct investment from a certification system to a reporting system in September 1998.

Meanwhile, residents' overseas equity investments began in 1985 by allowing securities companies' underwriting of bonds issued in foreign currency abroad by domestic enterprises. After that, the scope of eligible investment institutions and securities was gradually expanded. In 1994, foreign-currency securities investments by general investors were permitted. In 1996, the ceiling on foreign-currency securities investments by general investors was phased out, while the range of eligible foreign-currency securities investment vehicles was expanded.

In April 1999, the government comprehensively reformed the legal framework for foreign exchange and capital transactions to ensure their liberalization and to activate market functions rather than to regulate and manage such transactions. Instead of abolishing the Foreign Exchange Management

Act established in 1962, the government enacted the Foreign Exchange Transactions Act in April 1999. Consequently, almost all foreign exchange transactions related to overseas businesses for local firms and financial institutions were liberalized. In addition, the method of regulating capital transactions shifted from a 'positive system,' one that in principle controls them all but liberalizes them only in exceptional cases to a 'negative-list system,' one that in principle permits all foreign exchange transactions including capital transactions but prohibits only transactions on a negative list. These included safeguards to cope with emergencies such as sudden inflows and outflows of foreign exchange that may occur unexpectedly with liberalization. Specifically, a legal foundation was provided for the operation of safeguards, such as variable deposit requirements (VDR), capital transactions permission, imposition of obligations to hold safely, deposit or sell means of payment, and the temporary suspension of external payments and receipts.

Since then, the liberalization of foreign exchange and capital transactions has been expanded stage by stage, focusing on the overseas investments of local firms, financial institutions, and individuals. In January 2001, individuals' foreign exchange transactions including ceilings on overseas travel expenses, overseas emigration expenses and overseas deposits were liberalized. In June 2005, as the current account surplus persisted, there was a need to reduce the oversupply of foreign exchange in the local market, and facilitate the overseas advance of domestic firms by using part of the surplus. In response to this, methods of fostering overseas investments were introduced. For example, the investment ceilings on financial and insurance businesses per case by non-financial institutions were abolished, and the system of real estate acquisition by asset management companies was improved.

From January 1, 2006, as the capital transaction permission system was abolished under Article 2 of the Addendum to Foreign Exchange Transactions Act, all the remaining permission items for capital transactions were changed to reporting items. In line with this, additional measures for encouraging residents' overseas investments were implemented. Regulations on overseas direct investments by individuals and overseas real estate acquisition by residents were relaxed in January 2006. Limitations on the scope of eligible foreign investment securities for individuals were also phased out in March 2006. In June 2008, the ceiling on overseas real estate acquisition for investment purposes was abolished.

In the meantime, after the ending of the capital transaction permission system in January 2006, the reporting of capital transactions to the Bank of Korea was gradually transferred to reporting to foreign exchange banks or excluded from the scope of report items. Therefore, the number of reporting transactions has continued to decline. In May 2006, the government announced the "Foreign Exchange Liberalization Implementation Method" in order to put in place the "Foreign Exchange and Capital Liberalization Plan" ahead of schedule. Based on this method, the government actively pursued the internationalization of the Korean won and liberalization of foreign exchange transactions by residents. As the global financial crisis broke out in September 2008, part of the plan had to be put on hold.[43]

As of the end of 2012, the number of types of capital transactions that must be reported under the Foreign Exchange Transactions Act stood at 14, including borrowing of foreign currency funds by residents, issuance of foreign currency securities by residents, acquisition of securities from residents by nonresidents, and derivative transactions. Detailed types of the transactions are described in Table 6.1.

Unlike the items stipulated in the Foreign Exchange Transactions Act, in all seven items of the "OECD Code of Liberalisation of Capital Movements" are still regulated under the "Foreign Investment Promotion Act," the "Capital Market and Financial Investment Business Act," and the "Insurance Business Act." Their details are set out in Table 6.2.

With nearly all capital transactions liberalized, Korea's capital market liberalization is now considered to be on a par with advanced countries. According to a capital liberalization index[44] calculated by Jung Ryul Oh (2010) on a total of 92 items under the "OECD Code of Liberalisation of Capital

43 For example, abolition of repatriation obligation of residents' claims on nonresidents, gradual transfer of declaration of capital transactions from the Ministry of Strategy and Finance and the Bank of Korea to foreign exchange banks, and allowance of all FX businesses related to foreign exchange agencies.

44 Jung Ryul Oh (2010) calculated a capital liberalization figure for each country on his index by a simple binary method, which is to give one point on each item with no reservation, and zero (0) point on each item with reservation on the total of 92 items listed in the "OECD Code of Liberalisation of Capital Movements." Accordingly, the capital liberalization figure for each country is the ratio of the number of items with no reservation to the total of 92 items.

Table 6.1 Types of Capital Transactions Subject to Declaration under the Foreign Exchange Transactions Act

1. Some deposits and trust transactions in Korea, and some deposits and trust transactions abroad

2. Borrowing of foreign currency funds and issuance of foreign currency securities by residents

3. Loans to nonresidents by residents

4. Transactions related to the accrual of claims arising from guarantee contracts

5. Capital transactions arising from purchase and sale of means of foreign payment, claims and others, and service contracts

6. Derivatives transactions

7. Acquisition of securities from nonresidents by residents

8. Acquisition of securities from residents by nonresidents

9. Acquisition of overseas real estate by residents

10. Acquisition of domestic real estate by nonresidents

11. Other capital transactions

12. Overseas direct investments in offshore finance companies by residents

13. Payment of operating funds to overseas branches of non-financial institutions

14. Business activities by overseas branches of non-financial institutions

Table 6.2 Capital Transactions under Reservations to the OECD Code of Liberalisation of Capital Movements

Item[1]		Type of transaction	Details of reservation
List A	I/A	Direct investment	Restrictions on direct investment in designated sectors by nonresidents
List B	III/B1	Operations in real estate	Restrictions on acquisition of overseas real estate by a domestic insurance company (within 30 percent of its total assets)

List A	IV/C1	Operations in securities on capital markets	Restrictions on acquisitions by nonresidents of listed shares issued by designated public-sector utilities in the process of privatization
	IV/D1		Restrictions on purchases by a domestic insurance company of securities issued in a foreign capital market or with a foreign currency in the domestic capital market (within 30 per cent of its total assets)
List B	V/D1	Operations on money markets	Restrictions on the purchase by a domestic insurance company of securities issued in a foreign money market or in foreign currency in the domestic money market (within 30 per cent of its total assets)
List A	VII/ D1	Operations in collective investment securities	Restrictions on the purchase by a domestic insurance company of collective investment securities issued in a foreign financial market or in foreign currency in the domestic market (within 30 per cent of its total assets)
List B	XI/B2	Operation of deposit accounts	Restrictions on the operation of overseas deposit accounts by a domestic insurance company (within 30 per cent of its total assets)

1. Any item set out in List A in principle cannot be reserved again after the implementation of liberalization, but any item set out in List B can be reserved again according to economic circumstances even after implementation of liberalization.

Source: OECD (2012), OECD Code of Liberalisation of Capital Movements, pp. 93–95.

Table 6.3 Comparison of Degree (2009) of Capital Liberalisation under the OECD Code of Liberalisation

(Percent)

	Korea	OECD[1]	Emerging[2]	USA	Japan	EU	Mexico	Poland
Total	90.9	90.3	86.5	94.9	84.8	90.4	85.9	85.9
List A	89.1	90.0	87.0	90.9	85.5	90.5	85.5	87.3
List B	93.2	90.7	86.0	100.0	84.1	90.2	86.4	84.1

1. Excludes Korea.
2. Turkey, Mexico, Czech Republic, Hungary, Poland, and Slovakia.

Sources: OECD (2010), OECD Code of Liberalisation of Capital Movements; Oh (2010), The Present Status of Foreign Exchange Liberalization and Tasks Ahead in Korea, Bank of Korea, August 6.

Movements," Korea ranked on a par with the average of all 34 member countries, and was 18th with a score of 90.9 percent as of 2009.[45]

2. Korea's Capital Liberalization Developments

The scope of capital transactions at present can be classified as types of securities investment, direct investment, deposits, loans, real estates, overseas financing, derivatives, and others, taking into account the system of the "OECD Code of Liberalisation of Capital Movements" and that of domestic capital transactions. The "Foreign Exchange Transactions Act," "Foreign Investment Promotion Act," and "Capital Market and Financial Investment Business Act" apply to these transactions. This book covers only securities investments which have a large impact on exchange rates, equity prices, and interest rates in the financial and foreign exchange markets due to large volumes of capital transactions, and frequent inflows and outflow of foreign capital.[46]

Securities investments refer to equity and bond investing

45　The degree of Korea's real capital liberalization is estimated to be somewhat lower than the index calculated by the binary method, taking into consideration the point that procedural regulations on some of liberalized items remain.

46　Refer to Foreign Exchange Transactions laws, and "Foreign Exchange System and Foreign Exchange Market in Korea," Bank of Korea, December 2010, pp. 43–94, for the details of direct investment, deposits, loans, real estates, overseas financing and derivatives.

with the purpose of acquiring capital gains, dividend income, and interest income without participating in the relevant firm's business management. It is commonly referred to as portfolio investment or indirect investment. It can be divided into domestic securities investments by nonresidents and overseas securities investment by residents. Securities investment is distinguished from direct investment which refers to establishing overseas subsidiaries or acquiring a certain portion of firm's paid-in capital for participation in the firm's operations.

Domestic Securities Investments by Nonresidents

Changes to Investment System

In 1981, domestic securities investments by nonresidents (i.e. foreigners) were allowed for the first time through the issuance of beneficiary certificates exclusively for foreigners. In July 1984, the Korea Fund, the first international fund for Korea, was listed on the New York Stock Exchange with permission given for the purchase and sales of domestic securities by a dedicated foreign management investment company.

In January 1992, in line with the opening of the domestic stock market, nonresidents and foreign residents were permitted to buy and sell all listed equities (not prohibited in related laws) within a certain limit. Initially, the aggregate and individual ceilings per listed company were set at ten percent and three percent, respectively. But in cases of public business, such as finance, airlines and communications, and industry for which protection was necessary, the aggregate and individual ceilings per listed company were set at eight percent and one percent, respectively, while the Securities Management Committee (currently, the Securities and Futures Commission) determined the aggregate ceiling on a company which issued securities abroad up to 25 percent. Subsequently, ceilings on the purchase of domestic stocks by foreigners were gradually increased, and then abolished altogether on 25 May 1998. But, in the case of public corporations, such as Pohang Iron & Steel Corp (POSCO) and Korea Electric Power Corp (KEPCO), the aggregate and individual ceilings were limited to 30 percent and three percent, respectively. Pohang Iron & Steel Corp (POSCO) was excluded from a list of public corporations on 28 September 2000, and the sole such remaining restriction, the aggregate ceiling on Korea Electric Power Corp (KEPCO), was raised to 40 percent, while the individual ceiling was remained at three percent. Meanwhile nonresidents were allowed to trade stock index futures in May 1996, and stock index options in July 1997, respectively, on the Korea Stock Exchange.

The domestic bond market was opened to permitted foreigner direct investments for the first time in June 1994. Bond investment by nonresidents was allowed on listed convertible bonds without guarantees issued by small and medium corporations and government and public bonds designated by the Securities Management Commission. In the case of a convertible bond, the aggregate and individual investment ceilings were set at 30 percent and five percent of the total listed amount, respectively. Subsequently, the scope and ceilings of foreigners' investments in domestic bonds were gradually lifted, and on December 30 of 1997, all restrictions on foreigners' investments in domestic bonds were completely eliminated.

Any nonresident or foreigner treated as a resident who wants a guarantee of overseas remittances of securities investment funds must open an external account exclusively for securities investment as well as a nonresident local currency account exclusively for securities investment under his or her own name, in order to acquire or sell won-denominated local securities. Thereafter, they have to deposit or dispose of related funds. But, in cases when the International Central Securities Depository (ICSD) is entrusted with the purchase and sale of treasury bonds or monetary stabilization bonds by a foreigner, ICSD can deposit or dispose of the relevant funds by opening an account for investments under its own name. Where investment securities by foreigners must be reported to the Governor of the Bank of Korea as securities linked with derivative transactions, the ICSD is responsible for reporting them to the Governor. If foreigners intend to invest in securities listed on the market or securities registered in the related association, ICSD must be given an investor registration number (ID) from the Financial Supervisory Service (FSS), after registering with the FSS. In addition, any local investment broker and investment trader may open an external account exclusively for securities investments under its own name with a foreign exchange bank for the acquisition and sale of won-denominated securities or securities lending transactions permitted to foreigners.

On the other hand, no declaration is required under the Foreign Exchange Transaction Regulation in the following cases: where any nonresident acquires domestic currency securities through an account exclusively for securities investment; where any nonresident acquires any securities from any resident for foreign investment admitted pursuant to provisions under the "Foreign Investment Promotion Act"; where any nonresident who is of Korean nationality acquires won-denominated securities from any resident in Korea. Detailed cases are described in Article 32 (1) of the Foreign Exchange Transaction Regulation.

Except in cases where any nonresident can purchase any securities from any resident without declaration, any nonresident is required to, when intending to buy won-denominated stocks and equities of domestic firms not listed or not registered from any resident according to the object of investment defined in Article 2 (1) 8 of the Foreign Investment Promotion Act, make a declaration to the head of the foreign exchange bank. But these acquisitions do not have to fall into foreigner investment defined in Article 2 (1) 4 of the Foreign Investment Promotion Act. Except in cases described above, any nonresident is required to, when intending to acquire any securities from any resident, make a declaration to the Governor of the Bank of Korea.

Developments in Foreigners' Domestic Securities Investments

Domestic equity and bond investments by foreigners were partially allowed from January 1992 and June 1994, respectively. After ceilings on foreigners' domestic equity and bond investments were gradually increased, they were abolished at the end of 1997 and on 25 May 1998, respectively. The main features from the time of opening domestic securities markets to foreigners to the end of 2012 can be summarized as follows. First, foreigners' equity investment funds as a whole continued to show substantial inflows until 2004, while inflows of foreigners' bond investment funds were not large until 2002. Second, from 2006 to 2008, foreigners' equity investment funds flowed out in large amounts, but foreigners' bond investment funds showed sizable inflows. Third, since 2009, both funds have shown large inflows, apart from outflows of foreigners' equity investment funds in 2011.

More specifically, foreigners' equity investment funds continued to flow into Korea from 1992 when the equity market opened, but flowed out on a scale of 1.4 billion dollars in the second half of 1997. Foreigners' equity investment funds subsequently began to flow in again, registering inflows of seven billion dollars a year on average over seven years between 1998 and 2004. Foreigners' equity investment funds, however, started to flow out from Korea, selling for profit-taking due to the rise in equity prices; this volume of outflows increased sharply until 2008. Notably, the net outflow of foreigners' equity investment funds amounted to 28.9 billion dollars in 2007 and 33.5 billion dollars in 2008. This was attributable to increased risk-aversion triggered by subprime mortgage delinquencies, and the later worldwide deleveraging following the collapse of Lehman Brothers. But, in 2009, as the global financial crisis eased and Korea's economy posted a rapid recovery from the second half of that year, foreigners' equity investment funds began to flow into Korea again, registering 25.1 billion dollars in 2009 and 23.0 billion dollars in 2010. After outflows of 7.6 billion dollars in 2011, foreigners' equity investment funds flowed in again to the tune of 16.9 billion dollars in 2012. As a result, after foreigners' share of total stock market capitalization (based on the KOSPI) reached a record high of 43.9 percent at end-July 2004, it dropped to 28.0 percent at end-April 2008, and has since shown a gradually rising trend, standing at 34.8 percent at the end of 2012. As of the end of 2012, the outstanding balance of foreigners' equity investments reached 381.7 billion dollars.

On the other hand, foreigners' domestic bond investments were not large until 2002 although first allowed in June 1994. From 2003, they began to increase steadily. In particular, along with an expansion in arbitrage incentives, inflows of foreigners' domestic bond investment funds surged to 36.3 billion dollars in 2007 and 16.6 billion dollars in the first half of 2008. In the second half of 2008, foreigners' domestic bond investment funds flowed out on a scale of 12.6 billion dollars from Korea due to deleveraging during the global financial crisis. Since then, however, foreigners' bond investment funds have again continued to flow significantly into Korea, reaching a total of 45.7 billion dollars during 2009–2012. This was helped by the abundant liquidity of global foreign currency funds, positive evaluation of the Korean economy, and sound fiscal conditions. As a result, after foreigners' share of total domestic bonds registered 6.4 percent at the end-May of 2008, it fell to 3.7 percent at the end-April of 2009, and then rose again to 6.7 percent at the end of 2012. Foreigners' domestic bond investment outstanding reached 84.9 billion dollars as of the end of 2012.

Table 6.4 Trends of Domestic Portfolio Investment by Foreigners[1]

(Billions of US dollars)

	1995–1999 (yearly average)	2000–2004 (yearly average)	2005	2006	2007	2008	2009	2010	2011	2012	2012 (period-end balance[2])
Stocks	3.4	7.8	−1.4	−13.3	−28.9	−33.5	25.1	23.6	−7.6	16.9	381.7
Bonds	0.2	0.8	1.6	2.0	36.3	4.0	14.5	15.0	8.5	7.8	84.9
Total	3.7	8.6	0.2	−11.3	7.3	−29.4	39.6	38.6	0.9	24.7	466.6

1. Based on BOP; Figures of '+' or '−' represent net inflows or net outflows during period, respectively.
2. Based on International Investment Position (IIP).
Sources: BOK, ECOS; FSS.

Figure 6.1 Trends of Net Flows of Domestic Stock Investment by Foreigners (monthly), 2001–2012

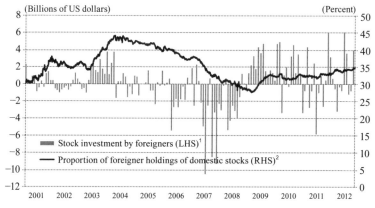

1. Based on BOP.
2. Based on KOSPI; proportions compared to market capitalization.
Sources: BOK, ECOS; FSS.

Figure 6.2 Trends of Net Flows of Domestic Bond Investment by Foreigners (monthly), 2005–2012

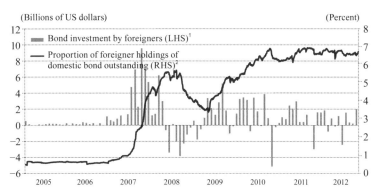

(Billions of US dollars)   (Percent)

- Bond investment by foreigners (LHS)[1]
- Proportion of foreigner holdings of domestic bond outstanding (RHS)[2]

1. Based on BOP.
2. Proportion compared to aggregate amount of listed bonds.
Sources: BOK, ECOS; FSS.

Overseas Securities Investments by Residents

Changes to Investment System

Overseas securities investment by residents was allowed for the first time in 1985 with the establishment of new regulations related to the participation of securities companies in underwriting groups for foreign currency securities. In accordance to this, domestic securities companies were permitted to underwrite foreign currency denominated bonds and depository receipts (DRs) that were issued abroad by domestic firms. At that time, the underwriting ceiling per securities company was set at one percent of the total issued amount or one million dollars. Subsequently, the scope of eligible investment institutions was broadened from securities companies to institutional investors such as investment trust companies and insurance companies, and the scope of eligible securities for investment and the underwriting ceiling were gradually extended.

In 1994, overseas securities investments by general investors such as firms and individuals were allowed, and investment ceilings per individual and firm were set at 100 million won and 300 million won, respectively. In March 1995, unlisted securities investments by institutional investors were permitted within 10 percent of the total issued amount. In 1996, overseas securities investments were substantially liberalized with the abolition of the investment ceiling for general investors and the extension of scope of eligible securities for investment. In April 1999, the establishment of offshore funds was allowed, and restrictions on the scope of foreign currency denominated securities for investment by institutional investors removed, while the deposit ceiling on resident accounts exclusively for investment in foreign currency denominated securities was phased out. In March 2006, investments for all foreign currency denominated securities were opened to general investors.

Investors under present foreign exchange transaction laws are divided into institutional investors and general investors. The procedure for overseas securities investments by residents differs by type of investor. An institutional investor is not subject to any prior restriction on the scope and procedure for investment, and is under only an ex-post declaration obligation. But in cases where an institutional investor buys and sells credit derivative linked securities (excluding acquisition as a foreign exchange agency), it must make a declaration on the details of the transaction to the Governor of the Bank of Korea.

A general investor is not subject to any limitation on foreign currency denominated securities for investment. But when intending to invest in foreign securities except collective investment securities, the investor must entrust the purchase and sale of foreign currency denominated securities to investment brokers (in general, securities companies established at home), and must remit investment funds abroad through an account exclusively for investment in foreign currency denominated securities opened in a foreign exchange bank. In cases where a general investor buys and sells foreign collective investment securities, the transaction must be conducted through domestic investment traders or investment brokers under Articles of 279 and 280 of the Capital Market and Financial Investment Business Act. If a general investor intends to invest in foreign currency denominated securities other than through domestic investment traders or investment brokers, the investor must make a prior declaration of the contents of the transaction to the Governor of the Bank of Korea.

In the meantime, no declaration is required under the Foreign Exchange Transaction Regulation in the following cases: where any institutional investor acquires overseas securities; where any general investor acquires overseas securities through an account exclusively for securities investment; where any resident acquires any won-denominated securities at home from any nonresident, who is a Korean national. Other detailed cases are set out in Article 7–31 (1) of the Foreign Exchange Transaction Regulation. For all transactions except for cases described above, any resident is required to make a prior declaration to the Governor of the Bank of Korea.

Developments in Resident's Overseas Securities Investments

Even though overseas securities investment by residents was first opened to securities companies in 1985 and allowed to the general public such as corporations and individuals in 1994, the volume of residents' overseas securities investments was not significant until 2000. It began to increase from 2001, and overseas equity investments by residents expanded steadily from 2002.

More specifically, the volume of residents' overseas equity investment stood at about 500 million dollars each year in 2000 and 2001, and then gradually increased. It expanded notably to 15.3 billion dollars in 2006 and 52.6 billion dollars in 2007. This was due to the fact that the ceiling on eligible securities for individuals' overseas investment was abolished on March 2006, and taxes on capital gains dividends accrued from overseas equity investments by way of indirect investment temporarily exempted in June 2007. But, in 2008, when the global financial crisis broke out, residents' overseas equity investment funds to the value of 7.1 billion dollars flowed back into Korea. Subsequently, residents again increased overseas equity investments gradually. In 2012, the volume of residents' overseas equity investment funds registered 14.5 billion dollars, with international financial market instability easing and global stock market recovering in the second half of that year. As such, they showed net outflows of 20.5 billion dollars during 2009–2012. As of the end of 2012, the outstanding balance of residents' overseas equity investments reached 93.9 billion dollars.

On the other hand, the volume of residents' overseas bond

investments, which stood at 40 million dollars in 2000, jumped to 14 billion dollars in 2005 and 16 billion dollars by 2006, helped by increased investments by insurance companies from 2001. But in 2007, the volume dramatically dropped due to the collapse of the US subprime market. Then in 2008, when the global financial crisis erupted, residents' overseas bond investment funds were repatriated to Korea to the tune of 16.4 billion dollars, as the National Pension Service withdrew investments owing to the decline of overseas bond yields and increased credit risks. Residents' withdrawal of funds invested in overseas bonds continued in 2010. But residents again resumed overseas bond investments, on a scale of 14.2 billion dollars in both 2011 and 2012. As of the end of 2012, the outstanding balance of residents' overseas bond investments stood at 36.9 billion dollars.

Table 6.5 Trends of Net Flows of Overseas Portfolio Investment by Residents[1]

(Billions of US dollars)

	2000	2001–2003 (yearly average)	2004	2005	2006	2007	2008	2009	2010	2011	2012	2012 (period-end balance[2])
Stocks	−0.48	−1.3	−3.6	−3.7	−15.3	−52.6	7.1	−2.1	−2.9	−1.0	−14.5	93.9
Bonds	−0.04	−4.0	−8.2	−14.0	−16.0	−3.9	16.4	3.5	1.7	−3.2	−11.1	36.9
Total	−0.52	−5.3	−11.8	−17.6	−31.3	−56.4	23.5	1.4	−1.2	−4.1	−25.6	130.8

1. Based on BOP; Figures of '+' or '−' represent net inflows or net outflows during period, respectively.
2. Based on International Investment Position (IIP).
Sources: BOK, ECOS; FSS.

3. Key Discussion Points

Korea has experienced two severe crises due to huge outflows of foreign capital. From 2009, inflows of foreign capital expanded greatly into emerging market economies including Korea upon the continuance of zero interest rate and quantitative easing policies in advanced economies. If foreign capital flows out on a massive scale, emerging economies may face such a crisis as those of the past again. Accordingly, it is argued that policy makers should routinely prepare methods to ease fluctuations in capital inflows and outflows to prevent crises. The following are some suggestions in regard to this issue.

Proposals to Restrict Foreign Capital Outflows

Some people advocate that policy maker should devise methods to stop outflows of foreign capital in order to avoid a currency crisis or foreign exchange liquidity crisis. If any country tries to stop outflows of foreign capital, however, foreign capital will shun that country. This, in turn, will make it very difficult for domestic financial institutions and corporations to raise the foreign currency funds necessary to conduct business activities or investments. Therefore, it is by no means easy to put in place measures to stop foreign capital outflows unless a country finds itself facing a severe economic crisis.

Under Article 6 of the Foreign Exchange Transactions Act an institutional basis is given for the Minister of Strategy and Finance to adopt measures to stop foreign capital outflows, such as a capital transaction permission system and a temporary halt in external payments in emergency periods. More specifically, the Minister of Strategy and Finance may, pursuant to the Presidential Decree, require any person who seeks to perform capital transactions to obtain permission, in cases where it is deemed to fall under any of the following cases: (1) where the balance of international payments and international financing face or are expected to face serious difficulties; (2) where the movement of capital between Korea and a foreign country creates or is liable to create serious obstacles in carrying out monetary policy, exchange rate policy and other macroeconomic policies. In addition, the Minister may temporarily suspend external payments where the Foreign Exchange Transactions Act applies, or on account of an outbreak of natural calamity, war and incident, grave and sudden changes in the domestic and foreign economic situation, and other similar events. But these measures may be taken for no more than six months unless special circumstances exist. And in cases where the grounds for such measures cease to exist, they shall be lifted without delay.

As described above, it is very hard for Korea to adopt measures to stop outflows of foreign capital except in an economic crisis or in situations where conducting macroeconomic policies faces severe difficulties.

Proposals for Responding to Foreign Capital Inflows

It is important for the government to adopt suitable methods to prepare for excessive inflows of foreign capital. Generally, methods to respond to inflows of foreign capital include sterilized intervention, the facilitation of overseas investments by residents, and direct/indirect regulation of capital inflows.

Sterilized Intervention

Firstly, sterilized intervention has limitations. The purchase of US dollars in the foreign exchange market by the policy authorities increases the supply of their own currency by an amount equivalent to it, and at the same time, the authorities absorb the increased local currency by issuing their own bonds. In other words, it is a method for a country's policy authorities to be able to absorb foreign capital flowing into the country without the expansion of the national currency. On the surface, it might look effective. Enormous financial resources, however, would be needed to absorb all the foreign currency funds flowing into Korea solely through market intervention.

There are limitations to raising the Korean won funds necessary for market intervention through the issuance of treasury bonds for Foreign Exchange Equalization Fund use or the Bank of Korea's monetary stabilization bonds. First, the government needs to receive consent from the National Assembly on the total amount of government bonds to be issued for market intervention every year. Second, it is impractical to issue government bonds or monetary stabilization bonds at will because overissue worsens the balance of the government's account and the Bank of Korea's balance sheet, assuming that interest rates on the government bonds and monetary stabilization bonds exceed returns gained from the operation of foreign assets. In addition, large issuance of government bonds and monetary stabilization bonds could induce a rapid rise in market interests by exacerbating bond market supply-demand imbalances. If the policy authorities rely on issuing banknotes instead of raising the funds for market intervention through bond issuance, it will increase inflationary pressures. Therefore, sterilized intervention should be conducted in a limited way, within the scope of available financial resources with the purpose of easing rapid fluctuations in exchange rates.

Facilitating Overseas Investments by Residents

Another method to counter excessive foreign capital inflows is the facilitation of overseas investments by residents. If residents buy foreign currencies in the foreign exchange market, and at the same time, buy foreign financial assets from the international financial market with them, the policy authorities can return the foreign currency funds flowing into the local financial markets without bearing the cost that comes with market intervention. On the other hand, in cases where foreign capital flows out from domestic financial markets, the supply and demand of foreign capital should be autonomously regulated through methods whereby residents withdraw overseas investment assets and, at the same time, provide the domestic foreign exchange market with the funds.

Even though this method sounds logical, it holds substantial risk. There is no guarantee that residents will repatriate overseas investment funds to Korea when foreign capital flows out from Korea. Nor is it easy for residents to withdraw overseas investment funds when needed because conditions in international financial markets will also not be favorable at the time. In addition, a rapid increase in overseas equity investments over the near term may induce increases in short-term debt for the national economy, and it may give rise to capital losses in case of a sharp drop in overseas stock prices for individual investors.

Korea actually experienced this when it encouraged overseas securities investments by residents. In June 2007, the government adopted measures to temporarily exempt capital gains taxes on dividends accrued from residents' overseas equity investment funds until the end of 2009. Through this measure, overseas equity investments by residents reached 52.6 billion dollars in 2007. This was a major factor behind the increase in short-term debt. However, when a massive amount of foreign capital flowed out from Korea after Lehman Brothers' failure, residents faced difficulties in repatriating their overseas equity investment funds because of a sharp drop in global stock prices. Considering this point, the government terminated the tax exemption measure at the end of 2009 as scheduled. Therefore, while it is difficult for the government to restrain residents from buying overseas securities at their own discretion, it is not good for the government to encourage active overseas securities investments by residents through tax incentives.

Regulation of Foreign Capital Inflows

Restricting foreign capital outflows, massively sterilizing intervention in the foreign exchange market, or facilitation of residents' overseas investments are not realistic remedies. Thus, regulating inflows of foreign capital is the only option to counter excessive inflows of foreign capital. Global consensus on the necessity to regulate foreign capital inflows has already been established through multilateral agencies, such as the G20, IMF and BIS, in the recognition that excessive inflows and outflows of foreign capital contributed to the global financial crisis. In November 2010, G20 Seoul Summit Leaders agreed that "in circumstances where countries are facing undue burden of adjustment, policy responses in emerging market economies with adequate reserves and increasingly overvalued flexible exchange rates may also include carefully designed macro-prudential measures."[47] This will be favorable to Korea, given its previous vulnerabilities.

Because domestic investments by foreigners have been almost fully liberalized, it is not easy to find a method to regulate foreign capital inflows. That is why it is best for the policy authorities to formulate a method to curb the volume of foreign capital inflows at an appropriate level or to regulate the pace of foreign capital inflows. Some economists have proposed variable deposit requirements (VDR), levy of capital transaction tax on foreigners' securities investments, and imposition of capital gains tax on foreigner stock investments.

First, Variable Deposit Requirement (VDR) require that some part of foreign currency funds be deposited with the central bank without interest payment. Some countries that have implemented a variable deposit requirement (VDR) system with the purpose of curbing rapid capital inflows are Australia

---

47   The G20 Seoul Summit Leaders' Declaration and the Seoul Summit Document, November 12, 2010.

(1972), Chile (1991), Colombia (1993, 2007), and Thailand (2006). Until the 1990s this system was evaluated to be effective in regulating the pace of capital inflows when capital liberalization was expanding in countries like Chile.

However, substantial negative effects—roundabout capital inflows for evasion of the regulations, the decline of foreign investor confidence, and the dichotomy of foreign exchange markets—were exposed. Some countries which operated this system more recently were not successful, eventually easing or abolishing the system before long. The Thai government introduced such a system on 19 December 2006, but the financial markets tumbled, with stock prices dropping as much as 15 percent in the course of the day. Therefore, the government excluded stock investment funds from the scope of eligible deposits on the following business day, gradually easing the regulations such as by increments in volume of funds eligible for exemption, and ultimately abolishing the system completely on 3 March 2008.

Second, a financial transaction tax can be levied on a certain ratio of the funds when foreign currency funds flow into domestic markets through securities investments by foreigners and overseas borrowings by domestic financial institutions. Brazil has responded aggressively with the introduction of a financial transaction tax when the Brazilian real appreciated greatly against major currencies due to surges in foreign capital inflows. Brazil imposed a financial transaction tax of two percent on real-denominated bond and equity investments on 20 October 2009, and it levied a tax of six percent on real-denominated equity investments, after two increases. But the tax was abolished on 5 June 2013.

Third, a capital gains tax can be levied on profits gained from the purchase and sale of financial products including equity investments. Advanced economies such as the United States and the United Kingdom impose capital gains taxes on profits from equity investments. Tax rates vary by country, based on the holding period of shares and the size of capital gains. Emerging market economies including China and Taiwan, however, do not levy taxes on capital gains. These countries have taken a cautious position on capital gains taxation plans, in view of the potential negative impact on the stock market. For example, China declared that there was no plan to introduce a capital gains tax in the future in November 2007, fearing equity prices would plummet. Taiwan also withdrew its own plans as the stock market experienced severe instability, falling more than 30 percent, after the government announced that it was considering introducing a capital gains tax on equity investments in September 1988.

Feasibility of Means of Capital Inflows Regulation for Korea

In Korea, a variable deposit requirement (VDR) system was established as a safeguard against crises under the Foreign Exchange Transactions Act, and a financial transaction tax on foreigners' securities investment has not been introduced yet. A capital gains tax on foreigner-owned stock investments is applied only to shareholders who hold more than a certain portion of the total stocks or equity shares listed on the Korea Exchange, and thus foreigners' equity investments are for the most part excluded from taxation.

Korea introduced the VDR system together with a capital transaction permission system and a temporary halt in external payments as a safeguard with capital liberalization under the Foreign Exchange Transactions Act (entered into effect from 1 April 1999). The Minister of Strategy and Finance may require anyone who performs capital transactions to deposit some part of the means of payment acquired in such transactions with the Bank of Korea, government agencies, the Foreign Exchange Equalization Fund or financial institutions. But the period of enforcement under this system, like the aforementioned capital transactions permission system, is confined to cases where the balance of international payments and international financing are confronted or at risk of being confronted with serious difficulty, and where the movement of capital between Korea and a foreign country creates or is liable to create serious obstacles when carrying out macroeconomic policies. This system may be put into effect for no more than six months unless special grounds exist. And in cases where the grounds for such measures cease to exist, they are removed immediately.

Regarding capital gains tax related to foreigner-owned securities investments, according to Article 119 (11) of the Income Tax Act and Article 179 (11) 1 of the Enforcement Decree of the Income Tax Act, incomes (capital gains) which foreigners gain by selling his/her equity stake are in principle subject to tax. But when a foreigner who holds less than a certain portion[48] sells his/her shares through the stock market, capital gains are not subject to tax. Accordingly, even though foreigners acquire capital gains through domestic trading, capital gains can be subject to tax only in cases when they hold more than a certain portion or the equities are traded over-the-counter.

Even though foreigners' capital gains on stocks may be subject to tax under the Income Tax Act, the National Tax Service cannot levy taxes on capital gains in many cases due to tax treaties with foreign countries. This is because under tax treaties including a prohibition on double taxation that Korea has established with many countries, in many cases, the authority to impose capital gains taxes is given to the foreign investors' home country and not the host country.

Therefore, according to the Income Tax Act and Tax Treaties, foreigners' capital gains on stocks are for the most part excluded from taxation. Capital gains on any securities (e.g., bonds) investments other than equities, however, are subject to taxation under the Income Tax Act.

Constraints remain when enacting or introducing the systems described above. First of all, because Korea is a member of the OECD, it cannot repeal any liberalized measures, as long as serious economic and financial disorder does not erupt, according to Article 7–2 of the "OECD Code of Liberalisation of Capital Movement." Variable deposit requirements (VDR) and the financial transaction tax may fall into this category. If Korea withdraws any liberalized measures already enacted, it must notify the OECD forthwith of its actions, together

---

48 A foreigner here refers to a nonresident who holds less than 25 percent of the total amount of outstanding stocks or equity shares listed on the Korea Exchange, in the year in which the transfer of the relevant stocks or equity shares takes places and throughout the period of the preceding five years.

with reasons, and will receive judgment on justification of its action from the Organisation.[49] But it is not easy for Korea to objectively verify that the action would comply with withdrawal requirements under the OECD's review. It should be noted that Korea may temporarily implement a VDR system in the event of an emergency under the Foreign Exchange Transactions Act.

The imposition of a financial transaction tax on foreigners' securities investments is a type of indirect method compared with VDR. But I believe it is not easy for Korea to introduce the tax in light of the following: (1) Korea has already been implemented some measures, such as the FX forward position ceiling system and macro-prudential stability levy system, to respond to excessive capital inflows. Additionally, an introduction of financial transaction tax on foreign capital inflows would, it is feared, induce foreign capital outflows from Korea; (2) discussions on a 2011 proposal[50] aimed at introducing a financial transaction tax throughout the EU received insufficient support within the Council. In accordance with this, only 11 of the 17 eurozone countries[51] among the 27 EU member states decided to introduce the tax.[52] Therefore, it is desirable for Korea to decide whether to introduce it or

---

49   See Articles of 13-a and 13-b of the "OECD Code of Liberalisation of Capital Movement."

50   That proposal involved a harmonized minimum 0.1% tax rate for transactions in all types of financial instruments except derivatives (0.01% rate).

51   Belgium, Germany, Estonia, Greece, Spain, France, Italy, Austria, Portugal, Slovenia, and Slovakia.

52   Council of the European Union (2013), "Financial transaction tax: Council agrees to enhanced cooperation," January 22.

not after an international consensus as to the introduction of a capital transaction tax has sufficiently formed.[53]

In addition, it would be problematic for Korea to levy capital gains tax on equity investments by foreigner minority shareholders, in view of tax treaties with other countries, and the negative effect on the stock market as well as the foreign exchange market. For the imposition of a capital gains tax on foreigners' equity transactions, treaties with other countries as well as Korea's Income Tax Act must be revised. In practice, this is out of the question because it is a task that needs a considerable period of time along with the revision of various bilateral agreements. Should Korea levy a capital gains tax on foreigners' equity investments, it would have to impose an equal tax on residents' equity investments according to equal treatment clauses between residents and nonresidents in these tax treaties. So if Korea announces a plan to tax capital gains on equity investments, this might cause a major disruption in the local stock market as previously seen in China and Taiwan.[54] Moreover, domestic equity investment funds owned by

---

53   In 14 February 2013, the Financial Times reported that, "While the Commission insisted the plan is legally sound, the long arm of the levy has raised the hackles of big investment banks, as well as the UK and Luxembourg, which rejected such an EU-wide tax. The US, which has long been opposed to a transaction tax, has also voiced its concerns. A Treasury spokesperson said the levy would harm US investors in the US and elsewhere who have purchased affected securities."

54   In Korea, a capital gains tax on equity transactions has been proposed by academia. In January 2006, with the stock market very unstable due to rumors that the government was planning to levy a capital gains tax on equity transactions, the Korean government denied it had any such plans.

foreigners can move to other emerging markets that do not levy a capital gains tax on equity investments.

In conclusion, the VDR system, a capital transaction tax on foreigner-owned securities investments, and the imposition of a capital gains tax on foreigner-owned stock investments are difficult to implement under normal conditions. Therefore, policymakers should find feasible and effective alternatives to curb the inflow of foreign capital without violating the OECD Code of Liberalisation of Capital Movement. Alternatives for adoption are the forward position ceiling system and the macro-prudential stability levy system, introduced in July 2010 and August 2011, respectively. They were enacted to enhance foreign exchange macroprudential soundness and are described in detail in Chapter 8.

Chapter 7

Foreign
Exchange
Prudential
Regulation
Framework

In emerging market economies, because a financial crisis tends to be led by the foreign exchange sector, foreign exchange prudential regulation plays a significant role. In particular, in liberalized capital markets, emerging economies with a free-floating exchange rate need to carefully manage foreign exchange stability in financial institutions due to the large risks from their currency and maturity mismatches.

In Korea, authority for foreign exchange prudential regulation of financial institutions lies with the Minister of Strategy and Finance. Part of the Minister's authority is entrusted to the Governor of the Bank of Korea and the Financial Services Commission.

This chapter first describes the definition and purpose of foreign exchange prudential regulation, and then briefly explains its framework in Korea.

1. Definition and Purpose of Foreign Exchange Prudential Regulation

The term "prudential regulation" refers to the use of various prudential tools with the objective of securing the soundness of individual financial institutions and maintaining the stability of the financial system as a whole. It is divided into microprudential regulation and macroprudential regulation. Macroprudential regulation has the purpose of stabilizing the financial system as a whole, while microprudential regulation aims to prevent the insolvency or bankruptcy of individual financial institutions.

The issue of a macroprudential approach began to be discussed among central banks and international financial organizations upon a more widespread recognition that the microprudential approach had limitations in the wake of the Asian financial crisis in 1997. More recently, the importance of macroprudential regulation has been highlighted following Lehman Brothers' collapse in September 2008, triggering a global financial crisis in a short period of time. In accordance with this, discussions regarding the development of macroprudential policy measures have taken place between the G20, IMF, Bank for International Settlements (BIS), and the Financial Stability Board (FSB).[55] In particular, the G20

---

55 The FSB was established in April 2009 as the successor to the Financial Stability Forum (FSF). It consists of member countries of the G20, international organizations including BIS, ECB, EC, IMF, OECD and the World Bank, and International standard-setting bodies and other groupings such as Basel Committee

Seoul Summit in November 2010 agreed that "in circumstances where countries are facing an undue burden of adjustment, policy responses in emerging market economies with adequate reserves and increasingly overvalued flexible exchange rates may also include carefully designed macro-prudential measures." As such, common ground over the necessity of stronger macroprudential regulation was formed.

Prudential regulation can be divided into regulation over the local currency denominated financial sector and regulation over the foreign exchange sector, based on the applicable currencies. In advanced economies, because their currencies are widely used around the world, and the separation of local currency denominated finance and foreign currency finance is virtually impossible, it is meaningless to differentiate the prudential regulation of local currency denominated finance from that of foreign currency finance. In emerging economies, however, where the financial crises often first emerge in the foreign exchange sector, its prudential regulation plays a significant role. In particular, in liberalized capital markets, emerging economies with a free-floating exchange rate, the foreign exchange soundness of financial institutions needs to be managed carefully due to the large risks from currency and

on Banking Supervision (BCBS) and Committee on the Global Financial System (CGFS). Main mandate of the FSB is to: assess vulnerabilities affecting the financial system, and identify and oversee action needed to address them; monitor and advise on market developments and their implications for regulatory policy; manage contingency planning for cross-border crisis management, particularly with respect to systemically important firms.

Table 7.1 Prudential Instruments of Foreign Exchange Sector

Type	Main instruments
Expansion of foreign exchange reserves	• Reduction of exchange rate volatility through FX market intervention • Accumulation of foreign exchange reserves
Measures to strengthen bank balance sheets	• FX position limits • FX lending restriction • Currency and maturity mismatches limit • FX liquidity risk management
Measures to influence credit growth	• Reserve requirements
Measures to control capital inflows	• Variable deposit requirement (VDR), controls on foreign currency borrowing, particularly short-term • Financial transactions tax on foreign capital investment

Sources: Committee on the Global Financial System (2010), "Macroprudential Instruments and Frameworks: a Stocktaking of Issues and Experiences," CGFS papers No. 38, BIS, May; Ramon Moreno (2011), "Policymaking from a "Macroprudential" Perspective in Emerging Market Economies," BIS Working Papers No. 336, January.

maturity mismatches.[56]

Instruments for enhancing the prudential soundness of the foreign exchange sector include an increase of foreign exchange reserves, tightening of regulations concerning bank

56   Allen, et al. (2002) insisted that "an analytical framework that examines the balance sheets of an economy's major sectors for maturity, currency, and capital structure mismatches helps to highlight how balance sheet problems in one sector can spill over into other sectors, and eventually trigger an external balance of payments crisis." Greenspan (2001) pointed out that "extensive short-term foreign currency liabilities of financial intermediaries that are used to fund unhedged long-term lending in a domestic currency are tinder awaiting conflagration."

balance sheets, limits on credit expansion, and restrictions on capital inflows. Foreign exchange prudential regulation of financial institutions in the beginning involved imposing reserve requirements on banking institutions, based on a certain fraction of their foreign currency deposits so as to respond to a sudden withdrawal of deposits by customers. But, as excessive foreign capital movements were identified as a main cause of financial crisis, even while foreign exchange transactions expanded, becoming sophisticated and diversified with the progress of capital liberalization, foreign exchange prudential regulation has been strengthened gradually.

2. Framework of Korea's Foreign Exchange Prudential Regulation

The authority for the foreign exchange prudential regulations of financial institutions in Korea lies with the Minister of Strategy and Finance. Under Article 11 (2) of the Foreign Exchange Transactions Act, in cases where it is recognized as necessary to maintain stability in the foreign exchange markets and the soundness of foreign exchange agencies, the Minister may impose restrictions on the raising and operation of foreign currencies. Detailed standards for such restrictions are prescribed in Article 21 of the Enforcement Decree of the Foreign Exchange Transactions Act. Part of the Minister's authority is entrusted to the Governor of the Bank of Korea and the Financial Services Commission under Article 23 (1) of the Foreign Exchange Transactions Act and Article 37 (2) and (3) of its Enforcement Decree.

The aspects entrusted to the Governor of the Bank of Korea include five items that are related to macroprudential regulation of the foreign exchange sector, and standards of business for foreign exchange brokerage companies and money exchangers: (1) setting of the minimum of reserves for specific foreign currency liabilities;[57] (2) setting of FX position limits for foreign exchange banks; (3) establishing methods of raising and operating foreign currency funds; (4) setting of standards for foreign exchange brokerage companies; and (5) creation of standards of foreign exchange business for money exchangers. With regard to the setting of FX position limits for foreign exchange banks, the separation and limits on overbought and oversold foreign exchange are stipulated in Articles 2-9 and 2-9-2 of the Foreign Exchange Transaction Regulation. As a result, the Governor of the Bank of Korea determines the definition of overbought and oversold positions, the scope of assets and liabilities as standards for calculating positions, the method of calculating positions, and the method of managing position limits.

Meanwhile, the aspects entrusted to the Financial Services Commission include five items that are mainly related to the microprudential regulation of foreign exchange sector:

---

57 The Monetary Policy Committee of the Bank of Korea, as the supreme policy-setting body of the central bank, recognizing the setting of minimum ratios as within its own authority, decides the minimum ratios of reserves which each foreign exchange bank must maintain.

(1) management of FX position limits of foreign exchange agencies apart from foreign exchange banks; (2) regulation of ratio of foreign currency assets and liabilities; (3) setting of offshore business accounts; (4) establishment of standards for the accounting treatment of foreign exchange agencies' FX accounts; and (5) creation of risk management standards incidental to FX business.

Chapter 8

Foreign
Exchange
Macroprudential
Regulation

The Bank of Korea's authority for foreign exchange prudential regulation, which is entrusted to it by the Minister of Strategy and Finance, is mainly related to macroprudential regulation. For example, the Bank establishes minimum reserve requirements for foreign currency deposits, sets and manages standards for calculating FX position limits on foreign exchange banks, and regulates the method of raising and operating foreign currency funds.

On 14 June 2010, the Ministry of Strategy and Finance, the Bank of Korea, the Financial Services Commission, and the Financial Supervisory Service jointly announced "New Macro-Prudential Measures to Mitigate the Volatility of Capital Flows" including the establishment of FX forward limits to enhance the macroprudential soundness of foreign exchange agencies. On 19 December of the same year, they also published a plan to impose a "Macro-prudential Stability Levy" on non-deposit foreign currency liabilities.

This chapter describes in some detail the characteristics of foreign exchange macroprudential instruments one by one. It then evaluates several measures for foreign exchange macroprudential regulation, and presents policy directions for its improvement in the years ahead.

1. Establishment of Minimum Reserve Requirements for Foreign Currency Deposits

Function

The reserve requirement system is one under which financial institutions are legally obliged to hold a certain ratio of their liabilities as minimum reserves in accounts with the central bank. The system was introduced as a tool to protect depositors. But from the 1930s, particularly in the USA, it came to play a more important role as a monetary policy instrument to adjust the credit supply of financial institutions. The system not only has a direct and immediate effect on the credit creation capacity of financial institutions by changing the required reserve requirement ratios, but also affects the funding costs of financial institutions because they should hold the required reserve requirements with no interest receipts in the central bank.

Reserve Requirement System for Foreign Currency Deposits in Korea

In Korea, the Bank of Korea's Monetary Policy Committee is authorized to impose minimum reserve requirements on foreign currency deposits as well as won-denominated deposits of commercial banks. The reserve requirement system for foreign currency deposits was introduced in the second half of

July 1967 as domestic banks launched full-scale operations of foreign exchange business with the creation of Korea Exchange Bank and the promotion of five commercial banks to "Class A" foreign exchange banks.

First, a quick review of current reserve requirement system for foreign currency deposits. Financial institutions that should hold reserve requirements in the Bank of Korea are foreign exchange banks under the Foreign Exchange Transactions Act. The liabilities subject to reserve requirements are all foreign currency deposits and certificates of deposit (CDs) of foreign exchange banks. Foreign exchange deposits consist of resident accounts, external accounts opened by nonresidents or foreign residents, and emigrant accounts which are opened by emigrants. For resident accounts and external accounts, there are five types of deposits; namely, checking deposits, passbook deposits, notice deposits, time deposits, and installment savings deposits. Emigrant accounts include all but installment savings deposits. Temporary deposits can be opened when the type of account is not clarified.

Computing of the minimum required reserves on foreign currency deposits and the imposition of penalties shall be conducted together with regulations on reserve requirements for won-denominated deposits. The minimum required reserves of foreign currency deposits are calculated by multiplying the daily average outstanding balance of foreign currency deposits subject to reserve requirements from the first to the last day of each month by the reserve requirement ratio. They should be maintained with the Bank of Korea within the period of reserve requirement calculation, based on the daily average outstanding balance of deposits, from the Thursday of the second week of the next month to the Wednesday of the second week of the following month. In principle, no interest payments are made on reserve deposits with the central bank. Reserve requirements should be deposited in US dollars with the Bank of Korea, but they may be held in Japanese yen for yen deposits. If a bank fails to meet its reserve requirements, the bank in question must pay an amount, denominated in Korean won, equivalent to one percent of the average balance deficient as a penalty to the Bank of Korea.

Developments of Reserve Requirement Ratio of Foreign Currency Deposits

Reviewing changes of minimum reserve requirements of foreign currency deposits, from the second half of September 1968 to the first half of November 1979, different reserve requirement ratios were applied to savings deposits (including time deposits) and to demand deposits. And then, from the second half of November 1979, a uniform reserve requirement ratio was applied to all deposits, without distinguishing between savings deposits and demand deposits. But as foreign currency deposits for resident accounts rapidly expanded, the reserve requirement ratios applied to them remained higher than those applied to foreign currency deposits of the external accounts, bank accounts, and emigrant accounts from the second half of July 1985. This was to restrain the sharp increase of residents' demand for foreign currency deposits to acquire foreign exchange gains during a period of the Korean won's depreciation against the US dollar.

Meanwhile, with the entry into effect of the Foreign Exchange Transactions Act from 1 April 1999, without separating bank accounts from other accounts, foreign currency accounts opened as bank accounts by domestic foreign

Table 8.1 Reserve Requirements for Banks

(Percent)

Effective date	Time & Savings deposits[1]	Demand deposits[1]
8 Feb. 1967	15.0	15.0
23 Sep. 1968	10.0	15.0
8 Sep. 1978	5.0	7.0
23 Nov. 1979	1.0	1.0
23 Jul. 1985	1.0 (20.0)	1.0 (20.0)
20 Feb. 1987	1.0 (4.5)	1.0 (4.5)
8 Mar. 1990	1.0 (11.5)	1.0 (11.5)
23 Apr. 1996	1.0 (9.0)	1.0 (9.0)
8 Nov. 1996	1.0 (7.0)	1.0 (7.0)
23 Jul. 1999	1.0 (7.0^2)	1.0 (7.0^2)
8 Apr. 2000	1.0 (2.0)	1.0 (5.0)
8 Sep. 2003	1.0 (2.0^3)	1.0 (5.0^3)
23 Dec. 2006	1.0 (2.0)	1.0 (7.0)

1. Figures in parentheses apply to resident's accounts.
2. Effective from 23 July 1999, a one percent ratio applies to resident's accounts opened by foreign exchange banks.
3. Effective from 8 September 2003, a one percent ratio applies to foreign currency time deposits with maturities of less than one month, foreign currency CDs with maturities of less than 30 days, and foreign currency installment savings deposits with maturities of less than six months.
Sources: Bank of Korea, Monthly Bulletin.

exchange banks and overseas financial institutions, were classed as resident accounts and external accounts, respectively. From the first half of April 2000, the reserve requirement ratios of resident accounts were lowered to be on a par with those of won-denominated deposits, while different reserve requirement ratios were applied to savings deposits and demand deposits, respectively. From the first half of September 2003, the reserve requirement ratio of foreign currency notice deposits, which are allowed to be withdrawn within a short period though classed as savings deposits, was raised, while a minimum maturity was given to time deposits, CDs, and installment savings deposits denominated in foreign currencies.

As of the end of 2012, minimum reserve requirements for foreign currency deposits range from one to seven percent according to the type of deposit. A one percent ratio applies to external accounts, emigrant accounts, and resident accounts that are opened by foreign exchange banks. Among resident accounts, a two percent ratio applies to foreign currency time deposits with maturities of more than one month, foreign currency CDs with maturities of more than 30 days, and foreign currency installment savings deposits with maturities of six months or more, and a seven percent rate applies to other deposits.

2. Restrictions on the Use of Foreign Currency Loans of Financial Institutions

Definition

Foreign currency loans are all those loans extended whose the contract currency is different from the local currency. They are mainly employed for overseas use, such as payment for imported goods and services, overseas direct investments, and repayment of principal and interest on external foreign currency borrowings.

Foreign exchange agencies that can currently handle foreign currency loan business consist of foreign exchange banks, merchant banks, insurance companies, and specialized credit financial business companies. The Bank of Korea can restrict the use of foreign currency loans in case it is necessary to maintain the prudential soundness of foreign exchange agencies This authority resides with the Minister of Strategy and Finance under Article 11 (2) of the Foreign Exchange Transactions Act and Article 21 (3) of its Enforcement Decree, but it is entrusted to the Governor of the Bank of Korea according to Article 37 (3) of the Enforcement Decree.

Changes to Restrictions on the Use of Foreign Currency Loans of Financial Institutions

With the enactment of the "Regulation on Foreign Currency

Loans" in November 1952, a foreign currency loan system in Korea was launched to support purchases of raw materials and equipment facilities. For a number of years, for the purpose of managing external debt, money supply and the exchange rate, foreign currency loans were allowed only to fund imports of goods or technology, overseas direct investments, and domestic machinery purchases. But the provision of foreign currency loans for use as Korean won-denominated funds was restricted. This was because of concerns about a rapid increase of foreign currency loans and the expansion of external liabilities as interest rates on foreign currency-denominated loans were more favorable than on won-denominated loans with nearly no exchange rate risk thanks to the fixed or managed-floating exchange rate system used until the mid-1990s.

After the currency crisis in the late 1990s, however, the progress of foreign exchange liberalization, with a shift to a free-floating exchange rate system and other changes in financial conditions, led to an increased need to resolve difficulties in managing the funds of foreign-invested corporations and in foreign currency fund raising by small and medium firms. In accordance with this, restrictions on the use of foreign currency loans were completely abolished. Thus, institutions involved in foreign currency business such as banks were able to handle foreign currency loans freely.

Foreign currency loans began to increase rapidly from 2005, centered around working capital loans for use as Korean won-denominated funds; and then the pace accelerated further in 2006. The excessive expansion of such loans resulted in a substantial increase in foreign currency borrowings from abroad (external liabilities), and increased pressure for appreciation of the Korean won by increasing the supply of foreign currency in the foreign exchange market. In addition, it was feared that yen-denominated loans would bring about a large increase in principal repayment burden, exposing borrowers to greater exchange rate risk. In 2006, policy authorities implemented unofficial guidance for foreign exchange banks to conduct foreign currency loan business, mostly for overseas use. But foreign currency loans for use as won-denominated funds continued to expand substantially.

From August 2007, the Bank of Korea limited the use of foreign currency loans to funds intended for overseas use or for manufacturers' domestic facilities investment. Toward this, the new handling or rollover of foreign currency loans to supply working capital loans for use as won-denominated funds was banned. But in January 2008, foreign currency loans for domestic facilities investment were again permitted for non-manufacturing companies.

Subsequently, with a sharp rise in the won/dollar rate and won/yen rate, foreign currency borrowers faced increasing difficulties. In accordance with this, the Bank of Korea allowed a one-year extension of the repayment period for foreign currency loans for working capital in March 2008, and further extended the period for an another one year in October, for foreign capital borrowers to be able to adjust the repayment period for the loans maturing after 2008. In addition, to help exporting companies subscribing to currency option products, including Knock-in Knock-out (KIKO) contracts,[58] the central bank allowed foreign currency loans for settlement of currency option products for the purpose of exchange rate risk hedging. This was because small and medium exporting companies faced increasing difficulties and high possibility of bankruptcy due to a sudden jump in transaction or evaluation losses, which in turn could undermine the economic activity. By December 2008, the Bank of Korea abolished restrictions on the repayment period for foreign currency loans for working capital that had been taken out before steps in August 2007 to limit the use of foreign currency loans.

The foreign currency loans that sharply declined in 2009 in the wake of the global financial crisis reversed course to rise again from the start of 2010. In the future, a rapid increase of foreign currency loans would occur, if the demand for foreign currency loans spilled over into borrowings for domestic facilities investment, in line with the sustained recovery of domestic economic activity, the existence of interest differentials between won-deniminated loans and foreign currency loans, and an expectation of appreciation in the value of the won. Excessive expansion of foreign currency loans for domestic facilities investment funds was expected to increase fluctuations in capital flows, bringing about rapid outflows of foreign capital with the outbreak of financial instability. It would also increase external borrowings. In addition, corporations could face increased exposure to exchange rate risk as a potential decline in the value of the won would raise debt repayment burdens.

---

58   Knock-in Knock-out is a type of currency options sold by commercial banks to allow exporters to hedge exchange rate risk.

In response to this, from 1 July 2010 the Bank of Korea limited the use of foreign currency loans only to overseas use to prevent an increase in unnecessary demand for foreign currency funds. Accordingly, foreign currency loans for domestic facilities investment were in principle prohibited. But, in the case of lending to small and medium-sized enterprises for domestic facilities funds, the Bank of Korea allowed the provision of foreign currency loans up to loans outstanding by individual foreign exchange bank at the end of June 2010, taking into account difficulties in foreign currency borrowings from abroad, and the necessity of fostering manufacturing industry through import substitution.

Table 8.2 Foreign Currency Loans of Foreign Exchange Banks

(As of period-end, billions of US dollars)

	2004	2005	2006	2007	2008	2009	Apr. 2010
Total loans	20.2 (1.3)	25.2 (5.0)	41.1 (16.0)	44.9 (3.8)	50.6 (5.6)	42.3 (−8.2)	44.6 (2.3)
Domestic banks	17.7 (0.9)	22.2 (4.6)	36.2 (14.0)	38.5 (2.4)	43.1 (4.6)	34.9 (−8.3)	34.6 (−0.3)
Foreign bank branches	2.5 (0.3)	2.9 (0.4)	5.0 (2.1)	6.3 (1.4)	7.4 (1.0)	7.4 (0.07)	9.9 (2.5)
Others[1]	0.1 (0.09)	0.08 (−0.02)	0.02 (−0.07)	0.06 (0.04)	0.08 (0.02)	0.05 (−0.04)	0.09 (0.04)

1. Includes insurance companies, merchant banks, and specialized credit financial business companies.
• Figures in parentheses represent increases or decreases compared to the end of previous year.
Source: Bank of Korea (2010), Reinforcing Regulations on Foreign Currency Loan Use, Press Release, June 23.

Developments

From 2005, foreign exchange loans of foreign exchange agencies including banks rapidly increased, centering on working foreign capital loans for use as won-denominated funds. Foreign currency loans more than doubled from 20.2 billion dollars at end-2004 to 41.1 billion dollars at end-2006, increasing by 5.0 billion dollars in 2005 and 16.0 billion dollars in 2006. In response to this sudden surge in foreign capital loans, the Bank of Korea took measures to restrict the use of foreign currency loans in August 2007. Foreign currency loans increased a mere 3.8 billion dollars and 5.7 billion dollars in 2007 and 2008, respectively, due to the measure, but the outstanding amount reached a peak of 50.6 billion dollars at the end of 2008. Thereafter, foreign currency loans decreased by 8.2 billion dollars in 2009 owing to the global financial crisis, but increased by 2.3 billion dollars between January and April of 2010, driven by a recovery in economic activity.

As of the end of April 2010, the outstanding amount of foreign currency loans by foreign exchange agencies stood at 44.6 billion dollars.[59] By institution, the outstanding amount at domestic banks and foreign bank branches accounted for 77.6 percent and 22.2 percent of the total, respectively, with 34.6 billion dollars and 9.9 billion dollars. That of other institutions including insurance companies, merchant companies, and

59 The Bank of Korea has not disclosed data on foreign currency loans since April 2010.

Table 8.3 Foreign Currency Loans, by Institution, Use, Currency, and Borrower Category

(As of period-end, billions of US dollars)

		2004	2005	2006	2007	2008	2009	Apr. 2010	Shares in total (%)
	Total amount	20.2	25.2	41.1	44.9	50.6	42.3	44.6	⟨100.0⟩
By Institution	Domestic banks	17.7	22.2	36.2	38.5	43.1	34.9	34.6	⟨77.6⟩
By Institution	Foreign bank branches	2.5	2.9	5.0	6.3	7.4	7.4	9.9	⟨22.2⟩
By Institution	Others[1]	0.1	0.08	0.02	0.06	0.08	0.05	0.09	⟨0.2⟩
By use	Facilities funds	6.2	7.0	9.3	16.4	24.4	23.2	23.2	⟨52.0⟩
By use	(Domestic)	(3.9)	(4.6)	(6.5)	(11.5)	(17.8)	(16.0)	(15.7)	⟨35.1⟩
By use	Working capital	9.2	13.6	26.2	21.9	17.9	12.0	14.0	⟨31.3⟩
By use	Others[2]	4.8	4.6	5.7	6.6	8.3	7.1	7.4	⟨16.6⟩
By currency	US dollar	9.9	14.1	24.5	31.0	31.7	24.8	27.8	⟨62.4⟩
By currency	Yen	9.6	9.9	15.1	12.4	17.4	16.0	15.5	⟨34.7⟩
By currency	Others	0.7	1.1	1.6	1.6	1.4	1.5	1.3	⟨2.9⟩
By borrower	Large firms	8.6	1.2	20.1	25.8	26.3	21.3	24.2	⟨54.3⟩
By borrower	Small & medium firms	10.9	13.2	20.9	19.1	24.3	21.0	20.4	⟨45.6⟩
By borrower	Others	0.7	0.2	0.1	0.04	0.03	0.02	0.02	⟨0.0⟩

1. Includes insurance companies, merchant banks, and specialized credit finance companies.

2. Represents foreign currency loans for the repayment of foreign currency borrowings, overseas direct investments, etc.

Source: Bank of Korea (2010), Reinforcing Regulations on Foreign Currency Loan Use, Press Release, June 23.

specialized credit financial business companies stood at 90 million dollars. By purpose, the outstanding amount of the loans for the use of facilities funds was 23.2 billion dollars (52.0 percent of the total), while that for use as working capital funds was 14.0 billion dollars. In terms of currency, the outstanding amount of US dollar-denominated loans registered 27.8 billion dollars (62.4 percent of the total), while that of yen-denominated loans was 15.5 billion dollars. By borrower, the outstanding amount of loans to large companies was 24.2 billion dollars (54.3 percent of the total), while that of loans to small- and medium-sized companies was 20.4 billion dollars.

3. Establishment of Foreign Exchange Position Limits

Definition

Foreign exchange authorities regulate limits on foreign exchange positions in order to induce sound business practice among banks and to prevent disturbances in the foreign exchange market as a result of heavily overbought or oversold positions. A foreign exchange position is equivalent to the difference between the outstanding foreign currency assets and outstanding foreign currency liabilities of a foreign exchange bank, and is classified in the following terms, depending on which is larger. An overbought position or a long position is when outstanding foreign currency assets are larger than outstanding foreign currency liabilities. Conversely, an oversold position or a short position is when the opposite occurs. A square position is when outstanding foreign currency assets equal outstanding foreign currency liabilities. According to the scope of assets and liabilities covered for computation of the position, foreign exchange positions are classified as spot positions, forward positions, and composite positions. The spot position refers to an amount equivalent to the difference between outstanding spot foreign exchange assets and outstanding spot foreign exchange liabilities, while the forward position is defined as an amount equivalent to the difference between outstanding forward foreign exchange assets and outstanding forward foreign exchange liabilities. The composite position is the difference between the total amount of outstanding spot plus forward foreign exchange assets and the total amount of outstanding spot plus forward foreign exchange liabilities.

A foreign exchange position system was first established for spot foreign exchange in November 1964, and managed with a spot position limit and a forward position limit, upon the permission of forward transactions in July 1980. Even in April 1981, when a composite position limit system was introduced, the spot position limit and the forward position limit continued to be separately managed. But in July 1998, they were unified into a composite position limit in order to ease constraints in the operation of foreign currency assets. The composite position limit was raised from 15 percent of equity capital at the end of previous month in July 1998 to 30 percent and 50 percent in March and May 2006, respectively. In addition, a forward position limit was again introduced in July 2010.

Composite Position Limit

The composite position limit for foreign exchange agencies is set at 50 percent of equity capital as of the end of the preceding month. The overbought composite position limit is fixed at 50 percent of equity capital as of the end of the preceding month, based on the aggregate overbought amount of each foreign currency. But in the case of the Export-Import Bank of Korea, it is set at up to 150 percent of its outstanding loans in foreign currency. The oversold overall position limit is set at 50 percent of equity capital as of the end of the previous month, based on the aggregate oversold amount of each foreign currency. Equity capital is defined as the total amount of paid-in capital, reserves, and unappropriated retained earnings for domestic banks, and as the aggregate amount of Capital A, Capital B,[60] reserves and unappropriated retained earnings for foreign bank branches. An overbought composite position is referred to as an amount equivalent to the difference when the aggregate amount of outstanding spot assets and outstanding forward assets in each foreign currency is larger than that of outstanding spot

60   See Article 26 (Fictitious Capital Stock) of the Enforcement Decree of the Banking Act and Article 11 (Operating Funds of Foreign Bank Branches) of Regulation on Supervision of Banking Business for definitions of Capital A and Capital B.

liabilities and outstanding forward liabilities. In an oversold composite position, the reverse is true. These are the methods for a net aggregate position as well as a shorthand position for the computation of composite position. The former is calculated by subtracting the aggregate amount of oversold composite positions by foreign currency from the aggregate amount of overbought composite positions by foreign currency. The latter is determined by taking the larger among the aggregate amount of oversold composite positions by foreign currency and the aggregate amount of overbought composite positions by foreign currency. Currently, the method of a shorthand position has been adopted for the computation of the composite position in Korea, with foreign exchange banks filing a report on their daily foreign exchange positions every month with the Bank of Korea.

The composite position limit system had been operated to enhance the microprudential soundness of individual financial institutions, such as the management of exchange risk. As individual financial institutions strengthened their internal controls over foreign exchange risk, however, it was difficult to recognize the effectiveness of the system. The composite position of domestic banks had been maintained around a square position. In the case of foreign banks' domestic branches, as the actual overall position was far below the limit, the system did not act as a real constraining factor in managing their positions. Moreover, under the composite position limit system, the spot positions and the forward positions of foreign exchange banks (and particularly, foreign bank branches) demonstrated extreme contrast, specifically in the large scale of their overbought position and oversold position, respectively. This contributed to the deteriorating macroprudential soundness of the foreign exchange sector by causing a surge in external debt, increased upward pressures on the Korean won's exchange value, and stark imbalances in the forward foreign exchange and swap markets. Foreign exchange banks could buy forward foreign exchange on as large a scale as possible, as they could borrow foreign currency funds abroad irrespective of the size of their equity capital. This resulted in an increase in external debt (in particular, short-term debt) equivalent to the purchase of forward foreign exchange. As such, the volume of external debt increased remarkably, and the structure of external debt deteriorated. In turn, this spread concerns over Korea's external payment capacity. In addition, as foreign exchange banks sold spot foreign exchange while buying forward foreign exchange to hedge exchange rate risk, excessive purchases of forward foreign exchange by them acted to increase pressures for the Korean won's appreciation in the spot market. As a result, the won/dollar rate dropped significantly in 2006 and 2007, to the point where the won was estimated to be overvalued compared with the equilibrium exchange rate, which reflects economic fundamentals. Meanwhile, the excessive purchase of forward foreign exchange by foreign exchange banks expanded supply-demand imbalances in the forward and swap markets, resulting in massive investments in domestic bonds by foreigners as the arbitrage incentive widened.

Forward Position Limit

On 7 July 2010, the Ministry of Strategy and Finance again introduced a forward position limit (i.e., leverage cap on bank's FX delivatives positions) system for foreign exchange agencies including banks in order to enhance macroprudential soundness in foreign exchange, while maintaining the existing composite position limit system. The forward position limit was set at 50 percent of equity capital as of the end of the previous month for domestic banks, and at 250 percent of equity capital for foreign banks' domestic branches under Article 2-9-2 (2) of the "Foreign Exchange Transaction Regulation." Nevertheless, the Ministry of Strategy and Finance can adjust the limit by plus or minus 50 percent if necessary to stabilize the foreign exchange market (e.g., excessive volatility of capital inflows and outflows). In addition, the Governor of the Bank of Korea may allow a separate limit other than the basic limit described above for one year for foreign exchange banks for which an excess position is recognized to be necessary. The forward position limit system came into effect from 9 October 2010 after a three-month grace period was given to banks to help alleviate their burden in reducing FX forwards exceeding the limit at once. Thanks to this measure, overbought forward positions by foreign exchange banks declined.

Between April and June of 2011, the Bank of Korea and the Financial Supervisory Service jointly undertook foreign exchange examinations of six foreign exchange banks, including both major domestic banks and the domestic branches of foreign banks, focusing on oversight of banks' implementation of forward position limits, with a view to easing excessive fluctuations in capital inflows and outflows. The finding of the joint examinations demonstrated that overbought forward positions had increased again, accelerating the expansion of short-term foreign currency borrowings in the banking sector. In response to this, the Ministry of Strategy and Finance lowered the forward position limits for domestic banks and local branches of foreign banks respectively from 50 percent to 40 percent and from 250 percent to 200 percent of equity capital, effective July 1 of that year. The limits were further lowered to 30 percent and 150 percent of equity capital, respectively, effective 1 December 2012.

Meanwhile, under the authority delegated to it by the Ministry of Strategy and Finance, the Bank of Korea decides the definition of the overbought forward position and oversold forward position, the scope of forward foreign currency assets and forward foreign currency liabilities, the computation method for the forward position, and management standards for the forward position. More specifically, an overbought forward position is defined as an amount equivalent to the difference when the aggregate amount of outstanding forward assets in each foreign currency is larger than that of outstanding forward liabilities. In an oversold forward position, the reverse is true. The scope of forward foreign currency assets and liabilities that is applied for the computation of forward position includes all currency-related derivatives, such as currency forwards, currency futures, currency swaps, currency options, and currency-related credit derivatives,[61] as in the case of the computation of composite position. For the computation of the forward position, the method of a net aggregate position, which is calculated by subtracting the aggregate amount of oversold forward positions by foreign currency from the aggregate amount of overbought forward positions by foreign currency, is adopted. This takes into account the potential increase of external debt equivalent to a net aggregate amount of forward positions as the introduction of a forward position limit system aimed to enhance macroprudential soundness by restraining the increase of external liabilities. The limit on forward foreign exchange position by individual foreign exchange banks is controlled by the Bank of Korea for each business day, on the basis of the moving average of daily outstanding forward position during the preceding one month from the immediately previous business day, taking into consideration the purpose of the system and the volatility of the forward position.

On the other hand, even though excessive trading in FX derivatives by some non-financial companies gave rise to considerable problems, financial institutions' counterparty credit risk management had been inadequate. To address the issue, the Financial Supervisory Service established new "FX Derivative Trading Risk Management Standards" at the end of December 2009. In accordance with these, from January 2010, FX forward transactions of domestic banks and foreign bank branches with non-financial companies were limited to a fixed ratio of a maximum of 125 percent vis-à-vis physical trade

---

61 In another words, an FX forward position limit is referred to as an FX derivatives position limit.

to prevent excessive FX hedging. By August of that year, the fixed ratio was lowered to 100 percent. But in cases where an upward adjustment in the fixed ratio is deemed necessary, prior approval is required from the Risk Management Committee of the individual financial institution concerned on a case-by-case basis.

4. Introduction of a Macro-Prudential Stability Levy

Background

In December 2010, the Ministry of Strategy and Finance, along with the Bank of Korea, the Financial Services Commission, and the Financial Supervisory Service, announced plans to introduce a levy on the balance of non-deposit foreign currency liabilities at financial institutions. This would be a preemptive macroprudential instrument to minimize economic risk caused by rapid fluctuations in capital flows, together with the introduction of forward position limit system and the end of tax exemptions on foreigners' bond investments.

Following this announcement, the government and the Bank gathered the opinions of interested parties. For example, a working-level task force of financial institutions was formed, which included the FSS, financial institutions, and other relevant agencies. The Foreign Exchange Transactions Act and its Enforcement Decree were amended on April 30 and July 25 of 2011, respectively, to provide the legal basis for the "Macroprudential Stability Levy System." The Bank smoothed the way for its implementation by supplementing relevant regulations such as revising the Detailed Rules on Foreign Exchange Business and the establishment of Procedures for the Operation of the Macroprudential Stability Levy.

On 1 August 2011 after a preparation process of about seven months, the Ministry of Strategy and Finance, and the Bank of Korea introduced the macroprudential stability levy for the purpose of heightening macroprudential stability, improving the structure of foreign currency liabilities, and strengthening the economy's capacity to absorb external shocks. In particular, the levy seeks to heighten macro-prudential stability by moderating the volatility of capital flows, which acted as one of the principal risk factors for the Korean economy. During the 1997 Asian currency crisis and the 2008 global financial crisis, Korea faced severe difficulties due to the abrupt exodus of foreign capital. The amount of capital outflows reached 21.4 billion dollars between November 1997 and March 1998, and 69.5 billion dollars between September and December 2008. But the low interest rate policy and quantitative easing of advanced economies in the wake of the global financial crisis have led to renewed surges of capital inflows to Korea.

The levy was the result of a broader international consensus on the need for macroprudential measures to moderate excessive capital flows. At the Toronto summit in June 2010, the G20 agreed on general principles for the introduction of bank levies. At the Seoul summit in November 2010, the forum reiterated the need for macroprudential measures to curb excessive capital flows. Among OECD member states, the UK, Sweden, France, and Germany had already imposed bank levies to reduce excessive bank leveraging and to expand their fiscal resources. The levy differs from capital controls,[62] which directly regulate capital transactions and related payments/receipts between residents and nonresidents.

Highlights

The levy basically applies to all financial institutions, but was first imposed on foreign exchange banks, including 19 domestic banks and 38 foreign bank branches, considering that they make up a major part of the financial sector[63] and have immense potential for the generation of systemic risk. Liabilities subject to the levy are the outstanding balance of banks' non-deposit foreign currency liabilities, other than tunnel accounts.[64] Foreign currency deposits, however, are exempt from the levy, as its imposition would place a double burden on them, given

---

62   A policy of imposing capital controls involves direct controls on prices and quantities when foreigners invest in domestic equities or bonds. Typical examples are ① taxes on capital transactions ("Tobin Tax"), and ② variable deposit requirements, under which some portion of capital introduced must be deposited with authorities.

63   As of the end of March 2011, their non-deposit foreign currency liabilities accounted for 96 percent of those of all financial institutions.

64   Payable FX spot, derivatives instruments liabilities in foreign currency, and accounts dealing with liabilities for government policy objectives are excluded from eligible liabilities.

the deposit insurance system already applies. The levy rate is set at between two basis points and 20 basis points, depending on the original maturity of the targeted debt instruments,[65] with a view to reducing highly volatile short-term liabilities and encouraging long-term, stable sources of funding.

The levy base is fixed as the average daily balance of banks' eligible liabilities for the year at each maturity. The levy payable is calculated as the levy base times the levy rate. The Bank of Korea notifies banks of the levy amount on the fourth month after the close of the bank's fiscal year. Banks are required to pay the Bank of Korea on the following month. Banks facing financial difficulties can make the annual payment in two installments. Resources collected by the levy are deposited with the Foreign Exchange Equalization Fund (included in foreign exchange reserve holdings), and used to provide foreign currency liquidity to ailing financial institutions during times of crisis.[66] If banks consider the levy has been miscalculated, they can raise objections within 15 days of receiving their levy notification. The Ministry of Strategy and Finance is in charge of the levy, while the Bank of Korea is responsible for collecting and managing it.

---

65 20 basis points up to one year, 10 basis points for over one year up to three years, five basis points for over three years up to five years, and two basis points for over five years. The levy rate may be increased temporarily up to 100 basis points, upon revision of the related regulation, at times of acute surges in capital inflows that threaten to destabilize the financial market.

66 European countries differ from Korea in that they intend to use levy proceeds to expand fiscal resources (U.K., France) or for consolidated funds (Germany, Sweden).

5. Key Discussion Points

Korea moved to strengthen prudential soundness in foreign exchange in January 1999 through regulations involving foreign exchange liquidity ratio, ratio of maturity mismatch between foreign currency assets and liabilities, and medium- and long-term foreign currency funding ratio to prevent the recurrence of a foreign exchange crisis like that in 1997. During the global financial crisis of 2008, all domestic banks observed the ratios, but they still suffered a foreign currency liquidity crunch. This implied that the microprudential regulation of foreign exchange targeting just domestic banks (i.e., excluding foreign bank branches) was not enough. To cope with this, the policy authorities established a foreign exchange hedging limit on individual corporations and introduced forward position limits for financial institutions.

Evaluating Foreign Exchange Macroprudential Measures in Korea

Korea established a foreign exchange hedging limit on enterprises in January 2010, and introduced a forward position limit system in July of that same year, while eliminating the tax exemption on foreigners' bond investments from January 2011. The government also introduced a macroprudential stability levy in August 2011. So far, Korea is considered to have responded relatively well compared to other countries. Specifically, the forward position limit system is thought to have settled down smoothly in the following points.

First, the system applied forward position limits to both domestic banks and foreign bank branches alike. Some analysts point out that a much higher limit was originally granted to foreign bank branches, compared to the limit on domestic banks. But it is difficult to characterize this as preferential treatment for foreign bank branches, considering the difference in the size of their capital. Relative to the preferential measures for foreign bank branches when applying the foreign exchange liquidity ratio and ratio of maturity mismatch between foreign currency assets and liabilities, the forward position limit system is much more sophisticated. The system is significant in that the total limit of buying forward foreign exchange by each bank is fixed in advance based on its equity capital. Before the introduction of a forward foreign exchange system, foreign bank branches could buy a very large amount of forward foreign exchange because they were able to make adjustments in positions by selling as much FX spot as possible, since they could easily raise foreign currency funds abroad through their inter-office account. At that time, some foreign bank branches were known to buy forward foreign exchange that amounted to several times that of the initial limit (250 percent of equity capital).

Second, there have been limited side effects since the system's implementation. Some have cautioned that the forward position limit system could lead to an expansion of swap market imbalances, non-fulfillment of firms' demand for foreign exchange hedging and an increase in foreign exchange hedging costs, and potential exit from Korea by foreign bank branches.

But these expectations have not been realized.

Third, the pace of inflow of foreign capital into the domestic bond market and the volatility of the exchange rate have more or less eased compared to the period prior to the system's introduction.

It is thought that the smooth establishment of forward position limit system is ascribable to the fact that it was implemented only after the Ministry of Strategy and Finance and the Bank of Korea had made thoroughgoing preparations over a period of about seven months for all related matters such as the setting-up of appropriate limits. In addition, it is thought that eliminating the tax exemption on foreigners' bond investments was an appropriate measure. This was because with the existence of substantial arbitrage incentives, the retention of tax exemption could have encouraged larger inflows of foreign capital.

A Direction for Improving Foreign Exchange Macroprudential Soundness

What efforts should we make further in order to improve the macroprudential soundness of foreign exchange sector? When excessive inflows of foreign capital persist, they should be restricted at an appropriate pace, while abiding by the following principles. First, the policy authorities should not damage the free-floating exchange rate regime and the basis of capital liberalization. Second, they should not control outflows of foreign capital that had earlier been invested in domestic financial markets. Third, because they cannot completely prevent inflows of foreign capital, the pace of foreign capital inflows should be regulated accordingly. Should policy authorities introduce a new method to regulate inflows of foreign capital, they must be careful not to give foreign investors the impression that Korea controls inflows of foreign capital. In other words, the policy authorities should ensure foreigners want to invest funds in Korea's financial markets by emphasizing market-oriented methods.

As inflows of foreign capital have slowed since 2011, it is desirable to firmly bed down recently introduced instruments such as the forward position limit system rather than to introduce new systems. With regard to the forward position limit system taking deep root, the policy authorities should respond in a timely fashion through accurate analysis of developments in inflows and outflows of foreign capital and the demand for firms' foreign exchange hedging. The forward position limit on foreign bank branches, which is still much higher than that on domestic banks at the present time, should be gradually lowered over the medium-to-long term. But it is not desirable to make frequent adjustments to the limit in the short term. As the total limit of buying FX forwards by each bank is fixed in advance based on their equity capital, foreign bank branches cannot buy FX forwards in large amounts. For this reason, it is all to the good if the forward position limit of foreign bank branches is naturally lowered without causing side-effects in the market. For example, if the actual ratios of forward position to equity capital in most foreign bank branches continue running below their maximum limit (currently 150 percent), lowering the ratio further will have only a minor effect on the market. And even if ceilings on the forward position of foreign bank branches are reduced in the coming years, a relatively higher ratio on them (vs. domestic banks) is inevitable, as foreign bank branches' business is based on foreign currency borrowings from abroad.

In the meantime, as a substantial portion of domestic bond investments by foreigners is linked to the forward market, the policy authorities should thoroughly analyze movements in domestic bond investments by foreigners and in the forward market. A substantial proportion (for example around two-thirds) of domestic bond investments by foreigners is known to be hedged through the selling of FX forwards. For this reason, appropriate adjustments of banks' demand for FX forwards can bring about changes in domestic bond investments by foreigners. Thus, when imbalances in the forward market expand structurally, that is, the sales of FX forwards by enterprises persistently exceed their purchases, the policy authorities will need to examine the further reduction of forward position limit on foreign bank branches. But in this scenario, they should beware of reducing the firms' actual demand for foreign exchange risk hedging.

As described above, several tools for restricting excessive inflows of domestic bond investment funds by foreigners and foreign bank branches' borrowing funds from abroad were put in place through the implementation of the forward position limit system, the establishment of firms' foreign exchange hedging limit, the elimination of the tax exemption on foreigners' bond investments, and the introduction of the macroprudential stability levy.

Meanwhile, increasing reserve requirements on foreign currency deposits and imposing regulations on foreign currency loans may be seen as among the options to improve foreign exchange macroprudential soundness. But they do not seem to be necessary at the present stage. This is because foreign currency deposits largely consist of export funds and import settlement funds deposited by corporations, while foreigners' deposits are known to be not substantial. Thus, an increase in reserve requirements on foreign currency deposits would not be helpful in regulating inflows of foreigners' investment funds. Apart from this, because the use of foreign currency loans has been limited since July 2010 to funds actually demanded for overseas use, there is little need to further tighten regulations on foreign currency loans.

Chapter 9

Foreign
Exchange
Microprudential
Regulation

The matters entrusted to the Financial Services Commission by the Minister of Strategy and Finance concerning foreign exchange prudential regulation are mainly related to microprudential regulation.

As weaknesses in the foreign sector of domestic financial institutions became apparent in the wake of the global financial crisis in 2008, the Financial Services Commission and the Financial Supervisory Service announced the "Plan for Financial Institutions' FX Soundness and Strengthened Supervision" to prevent the recurrence of crisis in November 2009, and strengthened the related regulations in January and August of 2010.

This chapter first describes the establishment of ratios of foreign currency assets and liabilities, the management of offshore business, and the establishment and operation of risk management standards. It then considers the argument that regulations such as foreign currency liquidity ratio should be applied to foreign bank branches.

1. Establishment of Foreign Currency Assets and Liabilities Ratios

Outline

The Financial Services Commission sets (1) a foreign currency liquidity ratio and a ratio of maturity mismatch between assets and liabilities denominated in foreign currency, (2) a medium- and long-term foreign currency funding ratio, and (3) a holding ratio of risk-free assets denominated in foreign currency in order to protect foreign currency liquidity risk caused by volume and maturity mismatches between assets and liabilities denominated in foreign currencies.

In particular, since 2010, the Financial Services Commission has considered the degree of liquidity (the ease with which assets may be liquidated) by allocating weights to each type of foreign currency asset when calculating foreign currency liquidity ratios, and it has increased the medium- and long-term foreign currency funding ratio in order to strengthen prudential oversight of financial institutions. The FSC has also established a holding ratio of risk-free assets denominated in foreign currencies.

Among the three types of regulations, those on the foreign currency liquidity ratio and a ratio of maturity mismatch between assets and liabilities in foreign currency are applied to domestic banks, merchant banks, financial investment business entities (securities companies, futures companies), insurance companies, and specialized credit financial business companies whose a ratio of total foreign currency liabilities to total foreign currency assets is one percent or higher.[67] Regulations of the medium-and long-term foreign currency funding ratio, and the holding ratio of risk-free assets denominated in foreign currency are applied only to domestic banks. Foreign bank branches, however, are exempted from all three types of regulations mentioned above, in reflection of their long-standing role in supplying foreign currency funds to the Korean economy.

Regulation through Foreign Currency Liquidity Ratio and Maturity Mismatch Ratio

Maturity Management of Foreign Currency Assets and Liabilities

Any institution handling foreign exchange business shall manage its assets and liabilities denominated in foreign

---

67   The number of financial institutions subject to compliance with FX soundness ratio requirements was 62 as of end-December 2010.

Financial Institutions Subject to Compliance with FX Soundness Ratio Requirement

(As of end-December 2010)

	Banks	MB	SC	Insurers	SCFC	FC	Total
Total	55	1	62	53	63	9	243
FX Agencies	55	1	57	47	37	8	205
Domestic FX Agencies[1]	18	1	46	35	37	8	145
Regulated Agencies	18	1	9	3	23	8	62

1. Financial institutions whose headquarters are located in Korea (i.e., excluding the branches of foreign institutions).
2. MB, SC, and FC mean merchant banks, securities companies, and futures companies, respectively.
Source: FSS (2011), Domestic Financial Institutions' FX Soundness Ratio as of end-Dec. 2010, Press Release, February 28.

currency by classifying them based on each residual maturity, and maintain the liquidity ratio in foreign currency prescribed in the related regulations. The method of classifying residual maturity, the scope of assets and liabilities, and the method of ratio calculation shall be stipulated in "Detailed Regulations on Supervision of Banking Business," "Detailed Regulations of the Regulations on Financial Investment Business," "Detailed Regulations on Supervision of Insurance Business," and "Detailed Regulations on Supervision of Specialized Credit Finance Business" by the Governor of Financial Supervisory Service under the authority delegated by the Financial Services Commission.

Remaining maturities of assets and liabilities in foreign currencies shall be classified into seven time-bands as follows: not more than seven days; more than seven days but not more than one month; more than one month but not more than three months; more than three months but not more than six months; more than six months but not more than one year; more than one year but not more than three years; and more than three years. And special exemptions in regard to the application of maturity of foreign currency assets and liabilities are prescribed in Chapter 1 (3) of Appendix 14 of "Detailed Regulations on Supervision of Banking Business."

Regulation on the Foreign Currency Liquidity Ratio

The ratio of assets having up to three months of remaining maturity to liabilities having up to three months of remaining maturity is generally referred to as "three-month foreign currency liquidity ratio." Domestic banks and merchant banks shall maintain the ratio at the level of 85 percent or above, and financial investment business entities, insurance companies, and specialized credit financial business companies shall maintain a ratio of 80 percent.

As of the end of March 2013, the three-month foreign currency liquidity ratio of 18 domestic banks stood at 108.8 percent, exceeding the guideline of 85 percent by 23.8 percentage points. This can be taken to mean that domestic banks were holding as foreign currency assets maturing within three months 108.8 percent of the foreign currency liabilities to be redeemed within three months. In addition, as of the end of December 2010, the ratio of merchant banks was 89.6 percent, higher than the guideline of 85 percent. Meanwhile, ratios for securities companies, insurance companies, specialized credit financial business companies, and futures companies stood at 123.4 percent, 161.0 percent, 130.4 percent, and 122.6 percent, respectively, all exceeding the guideline of 80 percent.

Regulation on Ratios of Maturity Mismatch between Foreign Currency Assets and Liabilities

Ratios of maturity mismatch between foreign currency assets and liabilities are defined as the ratios of foreign currency liabilities exceeding foreign currency assets to total foreign currency assets by term, generally referred to as "maturity mismatch ratios." Domestic banks shall maintain a ratio of liabilities exceeding assets to total assets, when the residual maturity is due within seven days, that is, seven-day maturity mismatch ratio, at the level of −3 percent or above. They shall also keep a one-month maturity mismatch ratio at the level of

−10 percent or above. Financial investment business entities and insurance companies shall maintain seven-day and one-month maturity mismatch ratios at levels of zero percent or above and −10 percent or above, respectively.

As of the end of March 2013, seven-day and one-month maturity mismatch ratios of 18 domestic banks were each 2.4 percent, 5.4 percent points and 12.4 percent points above the guidelines of −3 percent and −10 percent, respectively. As of the end of December 2010, seven-day maturity mismatch ratios of merchant banks, securities companies, insurance companies, specialized credit financial business companies, and futures companies were 6.3 percent, 17.7 percent, 29.4 percent, 1.4 percent, and 1.2 percent, well above the guideline of zero

Table 9.1 FX Soundness Ratio of Domestic Banks

(As of period-end, percent)

	2008	2009	2010	2011	2012	Mar. 2013
3-month liquidity ratio (≥ 85%)	98.9	105.1	99.3	104.5	109.3	108.8
1-month maturity mismatch ratio (≥ −10%)	0.4	1.1	0.3	2.2	3.3	2.4
7-day maturity mismatch ratio (≥ −3%)	3.2	2.8	1.2	2.3	2.7	2.4

Sources: FSS (2011), Domestic Financial Institutions' FX Soundness Ratio as of end-December 2010, Press Release, February 28; FSS (2013), Domestic Banks' Foreign Currency Funding and Liquidity, Press Release, April 8.

percent. This respective one-month maturity mismatch ratios of them were −3.5 percent, 15.3 percent, 27.7 percent, 1.3 percent, and 13.2 percent, substantially above the guideline of −10 percent.

When calculating foreign currency liquidity ratios and maturity mismatch ratios, the scope of foreign currency assets and liabilities is described in Chapter 1 (1) of Appendix 14 of "Detailed Regulations on Supervision of Banking Business." And when calculating the amount of assets in foreign currency, the weight is given in Chapter 1 (4) of Appendix 14 of "Detailed Regulations on Supervision of Banking Business," taking their liquidity into account.

Regulation on a Medium- and Long-term Foreign Currency Funding Ratio

The ratio of foreign currency funds borrowed with a maturity of more than one year to a foreign currency loans with a maturity of one year or longer is referred to as "a medium- and long-term foreign currency funding ratio." Under Article 65 of the "Regulation on Supervision of Banking Business," when an institution handling foreign exchange business makes foreign currency loans with a maturity of one year or longer, 100 percent or more of such loan amount (including securities held to maturity in foreign currency) shall be covered by foreign currency funds borrowed with a maturity of more than one year. However, this shall not apply where the outstanding amount of foreign currency loans is less than 50 million US dollars.

The scope and classification by maturity of foreign currency

(As of period-end)

	2008	2009	Jun. 2010	Sep. 2010	2010
Medium-to-long term foreign currency funding ratio (≥ 100%)	105.6	128.9	132.7	136.5	137.3

Source: FSS (2011), Domestic Financial Institutions' FX Soundness Ratio as of end-December. 2010, Press Release, February 28.

fund-raising and foreign currency loans when calculating the medium- and long-term foreign currency funding ratio are described in Chapter 2 (6) and (7) of Appendix 14 of "Detailed Regulations on Supervision of Banking Business."

Regulation on Holding Ratio of Foreign Currency-Denominated Risk-free Assets

Any institution handling foreign exchange business shall hold as risk-free assets denominated in foreign currency no less than the lower of either: (1) borrowings which mature within one year × 2/12 × [1 − the lowest rollover ratio]; or (2) two percent of total assets denominated in foreign currency (referring to foreign currency-denominated assets on the balance sheet for the previous quarter) under the provisions of Article 64−2 (1) of the "Regulation on Supervision of Banking Business."

The scope of "risk-free assets denominated in foreign currency" shall be bonds issued by the central bank or government of a nation whose credit rating granted by the internationally reorganized credit-rating agencies is A or equivalent thereto (hereafter referred to as "A grade"), deposit money in the central bank, corporate bonds of A grade or above, deposit money in financial institutions of A grade or above, or assets recognized as equivalent thereto by the Governor of the Financial Supervisory Service, under the provisions of Article 64-2 (2) of the "Regulation on Supervision of Banking Business."

The scope of "borrowings which mature within one year" shall be debentures issued in foreign currency by financial institutions, borrowings in foreign currency, call money in foreign currency, foreign bonds sold under repurchase agreements, or borrowings equivalent thereto under the provisions of Article 64-2 (3) of the "Regulation on Supervision of Banking Business." The "lowest rollover ratio" is the ratio of the relevant financial institution's amount of borrowings with maturities of one year or less that are newly procured during a month to the amount of borrowings with maturities of one year or less that mature during that same month, and it refers to the lowest average ratio over three months during a period determined by the Governor of the Financial Supervisory Service under the provisions of Article 64-2 (4) of the "Regulation on Supervision of Banking Business."

2. Managing Offshore Business

An offshore business is defined as a business that any foreign exchange bank operates for the use of nonresidents (including other offshore accounts) by raising foreign currency funds from nonresidents. Under the provisions of Article 2–10 of the Foreign Exchange Transaction Regulation and Article 66 (1) of the Regulation on Supervision of Banking Business, in the event that any foreign exchange bank conducts offshore business, it shall establish an offshore business account to book these transactions separately from other transactions. Funds transfers between an offshore business account and other accounts require the permission of the Minister of Strategy and Finance. But this provision shall not apply to funds transfers within 10 percent of the average outstanding amount of offshore assets in foreign currencies (referring to the average outstanding amount based on the balance as of the end of each month) during the immediately preceding fiscal year. The restriction of offshore accounts' funds to external use serves to prevent the domestic foreign exchange market from becoming unstable as other accounts exempt from limitations on borrowing bring funds borrowed from abroad into domestic markets.

Under the provisions of Article 66 (2) of the "Regulation on Supervision of Banking Business," funding methods in offshore business accounts are restricted to the following cases: (1) borrowing from nonresidents or other offshore business accounts; (2) receiving deposit from nonresidents or other offshore business accounts; (3) issuing foreign currency securities abroad; and (4) selling foreign currency-denominated bonds to nonresidents. Operating methods in offshore business accounts are limited to loans or deposits to nonresidents and other offshore business accounts, and underwriting or purchase of foreign currency securities issued by nonresidents.

3. Establishment and Operation of Risk Management Standards

A foreign exchange bank (excluding domestic branches of foreign banks) shall set up and operate its own internal management standards by such types of risks arising from foreign exchange transactions as country risk, large credit risk, foreign currency liquidation risk, market risk, and so on under Article 67 (1) of the "Regulation on Supervision of Banking Business." In addition, in case any foreign exchange bank intends to newly establish and alter its risk management standards mentioned above or to conduct foreign exchange transactions in excess of them, it shall refer the matter to its internal risk management committee for resolution under Article 67 (2) of the Regulation. The Governor of the Financial Supervisory Service shall also establish exemplary standards for each type of risk and may request the correction of the risk management standards of any foreign exchange bank if they are deemed inappropriate under Article 67 (3) of the Regulation.

In the meantime, any foreign exchange bank (including domestic branches of foreign banks) shall independently establish and operate standards to manage risks arising from foreign exchange derivatives transactions (hereinafter referred to as "standards to manage risks arising from foreign exchange derivatives transactions") under Article 67-2 (1) of the "Regulation on Supervision of Banking Business." The standards were introduced in 2010 to strengthen the management of credit risk to counter-parties of foreign exchange banks and to restrict excessive FX derivatives transactions of firms. Standards to manage risks arising from foreign exchange derivatives transactions shall include matters which the Governor of the Financial Supervisory Service determines under Article 67-2 (2) of the Regulation. And the Governor of the Financial Supervisory Service may request foreign exchange banks to revise or correct standards to manage risks arising from foreign exchange derivatives transactions, when it is necessary for the soundness of foreign exchange banks under Article 67-2 (3) of the Regulation.

4. Key Discussion Points

Regulations on the foreign currency liquidity ratio, ratio of maturity mismatch between assets and liabilities in foreign currency, and medium- and long-term foreign currency funding ratio had been implemented for a long time to enhance prudential soundness of foreign exchange sector of domestic banks. But as weaknesses in the foreign exchange sector of domestic financial institutions emerged in the wake of the global financial crisis in 2008, the Financial Services Commission and the Financial Supervisory Service strengthened their regulations on two occasions to improve the prudential soundness of the foreign exchange sector of domestic banks. There is, however, an insistence in some areas of academia that regulations such as the foreign currency liquidity ratio should be applied to domestic banks and foreign bank branches alike.

The foreign currency liquidity ratio has yet to be applied to foreign bank branches, and this is because they have served as a channel for raising foreign currency funds necessary for the economy. Foreign bank branches have largely raised foreign currency funds abroad in the short term and have provided them to domestic financial markets through foreign currency loans and FX or currency swaps. As of the end of December 2012, the total outstanding value of their foreign currency funds raised abroad reached 62.3 billion dollars, which consisted of 36.1 billion dollars in short-term funds and 26.2 billion dollars in long-term funds. This is equivalent to 33.9 percent of the total external liabilities of all foreign exchange banks.

Given these realities, it will be difficult for policy authorities to apply regulations such as the foreign currency liquidity ratio on foreign bank branches in the near term. This is because it would create significant unrest in the financial system and in practices established over the long term. If policy authorities decide to apply such regulations to foreign bank branches in the near term, they will only achieve the reduction of a substantial portion of the foreign currency funds provided to domestic banks and firms as well as funds invested in domestic bonds. In this event, it may throw the domestic financial and foreign exchange markets into turmoil due to a supply-demand mismatch in the foreign exchange market. In particular, should foreign bank branches transfer their long-term operating assets into short-term operating assets, domestic banks and firms will face significant difficulties in managing foreign currency liquidity. Consequently, introducing regulations such as the foreign currency liquidity ratio on foreign bank branches will give rise to market disorder rather than systemic improvements. Therefore, it is desirable that this issue be reviewed over the medium-to-long term.

Policy authorities should carefully prepare a detailed action plan for the imposition of regulations such as the foreign currency liquidity ratio on foreign bank branches, and a supplementary plan for the side-effects expected from their imposition. But the introduction of regulations on foreign bank branches should be dealt with gradually over the medium and long term, considering the domestic foreign exchange and swap markets' capacity to absorb shocks. In addition, it will be difficult to apply the same foreign currency liquidity ratios to foreign bank branches as to domestic banks, such as the forward position limit system.

If the introduction of similar regulations on foreign bank branches is brought into effect over the medium and long term, the framework can be divided into three steps. First, it is desirable to begin with the lowest level. The lowest level means finding a level for the foreign currency liquidity ratio that almost all foreign bank branches can observe. In that case, some may advance the opposing opinion that it is meaningless to apply regulations such as foreign currency liquidity ratio to foreign bank branches. But in the first stage, it will be important to introduce the same regulations for foreign bank branches as imposed on domestic banks. This is because the regulations regarding foreign bank branches are being introduced at their lowest setting, the situation of foreign bank branches in terms of currency and maturity mismatches will not be worse than before. Second, regulations such as a foreign currency liquidity ratio for foreign bank branches should be gradually strengthened, based on the effect of the regulations. Lastly, the foreign currency liquidity ratio on foreign bank branches, for example, should reach a certain level. But it is not necessary to pitch regulations such as foreign currency liquidity ratio on foreign bank branches at the same level as those placed on domestic banks. This is because it is necessary to acknowledge the special characteristics of foreign bank branches, just as with the forward position limit system.

Chapter 10

Policy
Tasks
Ahead

Korea has taken measures to strengthen the prudential soundness of the foreign exchange sector in response to changing conditions at home and abroad since the global financial crisis.

These efforts should be continued in the years ahead. Medium- and long-term policy tasks must focus on restraining excessive inflows of foreign capital, and on reducing currency and maturity mismatches between foreign currency assets and liabilities. The improvement of related systems should be gradually pursued without causing "side effects" in the financial and foreign exchange markets.

This chapter presents several tasks that policymakers should press ahead with in the coming years.

1. Basic Direction for Improvement of Foreign Exchange Policy

Korea introduced several regulations, such as a ratio of maturity mismatch between foreign currency assets and liabilities, and a medium- and long-term foreign currency funding ratio for domestic banks in January 1999, to strengthen the prudential soundness of the foreign exchange sector after the 1997 currency crisis. During the global financial crisis of 2008, all domestic banks closely observed the ratios.

Even so, domestic banks at that time experienced a foreign currency liquidity crisis amidst a rapid rise in the won/ dollar exchange rate and severe instability in foreign currency funding due to global deleveraging. Korea's two foreign currency liquidity crises erupted due to sudden and massive outflows of foreign capital, suggesting that foreign exchange microprudential regulation of domestic banks alone (excluding foreign bank branches) was not enough. Thus, foreign exchange macroprudential regulations were needed to control excessive inflows of foreign capital.

A consensus over stronger macroprudential regulation was formed among the G20, IMF, and BIS. In response to recent conditions at home and abroad, Korea has taken steps to enhance the prudential soundness of foreign exchange agencies. These efforts should be continued in the years ahead.

Specifically, medium- and long-term policy tasks should focus on restricting excessive inflows of foreign capital, and on mitigating structural currency and maturity mismatches between foreign currency assets and liabilities. This is because

Korea like other newly emerging markets faces limitations in its role as lender of last resort in foreign exchange. Changes to related systems should be put in place through detailed research and analysis. This is because as the systems and practices related to foreign exchange have been established over a long period of time, any changes in the short term may create severe unrest in financial and foreign exchange markets rather than the systemic improvements initially intended. Therefore, improvements of related systems should be gradually implemented so as to avoid "side effects" in the financial and foreign exchange markets.

2. Several Tasks for Improvement of Foreign Exchange Policy

Policymakers should press ahead with the following tasks in the coming years. The first task is to release more data on foreign exchange statistics. For example, it is advisable to publish more data on a monthly or quarterly basis, such as the ratio of the composite position or forward position to the equity capital of commercial banks; foreign currency loans by institutional category, purpose, currency, and borrower type; and foreign currency deposits by currency and depositor type. The "institutional category" referred to above does not mean the individual bank, but categories such as domestic banks or foreign bank branches.

The release of more copious statistical data is desirable in the sense that policymakers provide more services to the private sector. It is also good in that the private sector can provide more realistic proposals to policymakers, based on broader opportunities to access foreign exchange information. When policymakers disclose statistical data on foreign exchange to the public, they must beware of revealing the data of individual financial institutions. This is because individual financial institutions may be exposed to reputation risk, and thus face difficulties in business management.

The second task is to strengthen policymakers' monitoring and analysis of foreign exchange developments. In doing this, it is important to identify changes in trends, and judge whether changing trends are structural or temporary. This is because different remedies should be prescribed according to the diagnosis. But it is not easy to grasp such changes in foreign exchange movements.

In this respect, analysts must not only have deep theoretical knowledge but also abundant practical experience with the economy as well as finance. Based on this, they can make prompt and accurate diagnoses, and then prescribe the most appropriate remedies in the particular circumstances. If an imbalance in foreign exchange sector is temporary, policymakers can resolve it by increasing the supply of foreign currency funds in the short term. But if the imbalance is structural, policymakers must elaborate more suitable remedies for systemic improvements rather than increase the supply of foreign currency funds because it is impossible to repeatedly provide foreign currency funds over a long period. For example of what is meant, we can cite up the forward position limit system introduced in July 2010 to improve the structural imbalance in the FX forward market.

The third is to improve the method of supplying foreign currency liquidity from swap market participation through agent banks to a more market-oriented, competitive swap auction. Since September 2007, the Bank of Korea has been understood to participate in the swap market from time to time, depending on foreign currency fund market conditions, to reduce imbalances in the market. It is desirable that current swap market participation method gradually shift to a competitive swap auction method in the near future. But until the swap market imbalance is substantially reduced, the Bank of Korea needs to conduct a competitive swap auction method in tandem with the participation method.

Introduction of a competitive swap auction method is expected to give rise to the following positive outcomes. First, this may enhance the predictability and efficiency of the Bank of Korea's foreign currency liquidity supply. It may also help eliminate misperceptions among market participants that the Bank makes insufficient efforts to alleviate swap market imbalances, despite the steady increase in foreign exchange reserves. This method may also weaken the insistence of some market participants that the Bank should extend the use of foreign exchange reserves. Finally, this method may not only produce a signal effect through the disclosure of bidding amounts, but it can help the Bank receive information on the foreign currency funding situations of individual financial institutions and the overall swap market.

The fourth task is to unremittingly exercise thoroughgoing management of the official foreign exchange reserves. IMF and international credit rating agencies have been giving positive assessments of current level of Korea's reserves. Unless the US-dollar translation values of currencies other than the US dollar depreciate sharply, the volume of Korea's foreign exchange reserves is expected to steadily expand thanks to interest income and market intervention through smoothing operations to mitigate rapid changes in won/dollar exchange rate. Therefore, their thorough management is a more critical task than an intentional increase in them.

The past two crises abundantly confirmed that sufficient accumulation and thorough management of foreign exchange reserves are very important. We must not forget this vital lesson. In the years ahead, it will be even more difficult to predict in advance when, where and what type of financial crisis may break out.

But if the volume of reserve assets continues to expand substantially, some economists may advocate the case for investing part of them to support domestic financial institutions and enterprises or to develop overseas natural resources. But the volume of foreign exchange reserves in a country is a result of its foreign exchange policy. Thus, it is not easy to assess whether the current level of reserves is appropriate or not. Moreover, international financial organizations have yet to present a uniform, global standard to assess whether a country's foreign exchange reserves are sufficient.

Therefore, I believe that judging the adequacy of foreign exchange reserves should be determined by policy authorities. And in light of their role as a contingency fund, even if the level is deemed higher than necessary, it seems proper for a country to hold foreign exchange reserves in the form of external assets with a high degree of safety and liquidity than long-term fixed assets during ordinary periods. It does not seem appropriate for the policy authorities to invest the reserve assets in the development of overseas natural resources or infrastructure projects because the investment funds would be locked in for a long period and with high risk to the principal invested.

Meanwhile, some argue that the Bank of Korea should invest its foreign exchange reserves in high yielding foreign currency assets, though the risk is also higher compared with government bonds, in order to strike a balance between the costs and benefits of holding them.

However, when investing reserve assets, the priority should be placed on safety rather than on profitability. This is a natural conclusion if we look back on the fact that some sections of the overseas media raised doubts about the immediate availability of Korea's foreign exchange reserves at the time of the global financial crisis. As such, sufficient accumulation of foreign exchange reserves is necessary to respond to an unexpected crisis, while the costs of holding such reserves are an inevitable result of policy.

Even though individual countries held adequate foreign exchange reserves, the individual efforts of each country proved to be limited in coping with the global financial crisis following Lehman Brothers' failure in September 2008. Therefore, Korea should work energetically to strengthen regional financial safety nets such as the CMIM launched in March 2010. At the same time, Korea should take an active role in discussions regarding the establishment of global financial safety nets at G20 summits.

The fifth task is to make continuous efforts to improve the macroprudential soundness of banks' foreign exchange sector. What is essential here is to reduce volatility from foreign capital flows. More specifically, it is to restrain excessive inflows of foreign capital at an appropriate pace.

Since 2010, instruments have been acquired for restricting excessive inflows of foreign capital from abroad with the imposition of forward position limits, the setting of firms' foreign exchange hedging limits, the introduction of the macro-prudential stability levy, and the elimination of tax exemption on foreigners' bond investments. Accordingly, the macroprudential soundness of banks' foreign exchange sector has been greatly enhanced from that in the past. So far, Korea is assessed as having responded relatively well compared to other countries.

In the years ahead, policy efforts for systemic improvements should be sustained to alleviate structural imbalances in supply and demand in the foreign exchange market. Above all, it is more desirable to bed down the systems introduced recently such as the forward position limit rather than introduce new instruments at the present time.

With regard to this, the forward position limit on foreign bank branches that is much higher than that of domestic banks should be gradually lowered over the medium to long term through accurate analysis of developments in inflows and outflows of foreign capital and in the demand for firms' foreign exchange hedging. But it is not desirable to make frequent adjustments to the limit in the short term. As the total limit for buying FX forwards for each bank is fixed in advance based on its equity capital, it will be better if the forward position limit of foreign bank branches can be lowered naturally without causing side effects in the market. Even if ceilings on the forward positions of foreign bank branches are reduced in the future, higher ratios for them (vs. domestic banks) cannot but be maintained, when we consider the special characteristics of foreign bank branches in that the basis for their business operations is foreign currency borrowings from abroad.

In the coming years, if there is a structural expansion of forward market imbalance; that is, the sales of FX forwards by corporations come to greatly exceed their purchases, the policy authorities will need to consider accelerating the reduction of forward position limits for both domestic banks and foreign bank branches, as well as the lowering of firms' foreign exchange hedging limit. But in this scenario, they should be careful not to shrink firms' real demand for foreign exchange hedging.

With regard to the imposition of a financial transaction tax on foreigners' securities investments, I believe it is difficult for Korea to introduce such a tax at the present time, considering the following: (1) Korea has already taken some measures, such as the FX forward position ceilings and macro-prudential stability levy, to respond to excessive capital inflows. Additionally, introduction of a financial transaction tax on foreign capital inflows could induce foreign capital outflows from Korea. (2) At the present time, only 11 eurozone countries among the 27 EU member states have decided to introduce the tax, while the United States and the United Kingdom are reluctant to accept it. Therefore, it is desirable for Korea to defer a decision on whether to introduce it or not until a more substantial global consensus has been formed.

The final task is to enhance microprudential soundness of banks' foreign exchange business. The core of this is to reduce currency and maturity mismatches between the foreign-currency assets and liabilities of individual banks. The same regulations concerning foreign currency liquidity ratio, ratio of maturity mismatch between assets and liabilities in foreign currency, and medium- and long-term foreign currency funding ratio would be applied to foreign bank branches as well as to domestic banks, as in the case of forward position limits. But this is a very sensitive issue that could bring about rapid capital outflows from foreign bank branches. Whenever this issue emerged in the past, domestic swap markets turned unstable, and their imbalances became accentuated.

Until now, foreign bank branches have been a channel to raise foreign currency funds needed in the economy. In light of this reality, it will be difficult to apply the foreign currency liquidity ratio and other ratios to foreign bank branches in the near term. Foreign bank branches have largely raised foreign currency funds from abroad for the short term and have provided them to domestic financial markets through foreign currency loans and swap markets.

Given these realities, if the policy authorities decide to apply such regulations to foreign bank branches in the near term, they will achieve nothing other than bringing about the repatriation of a substantial proportion of the foreign currency funds provided to domestic banks and firms as well as the exit of investment funds from domestic bond market. In this event, it may trigger severe unrest in the local financial and foreign exchange markets due to a supply and demand mismatch in the foreign exchange market. If so, imposing regulations such as the foreign currency liquidity ratio and other ratios on foreign bank branches will give rise to higher costs such as market disorder rather than bringing the benefits of systemic improvements. Therefore, it is desirable that this issue be reviewed over the medium-to-long term.

The policy authorities should meticulously prepare a detailed action plan for regulations such as the foreign currency liquidity ratio and other ratios on foreign bank branches, and a supplementary plan to respond to effects expected from the implementation of these new regulations. Then, the introduction of regulations on foreign bank branches should be proceeded with gradually over the medium- and long-term, based on the capacity of domestic foreign exchange and swap markets to absorb shocks.

If the introduction of regulations on foreign bank branches is put into action over the medium- and long-term, the framework can be divided into three steps. First, it is desirable to begin at the lowest level. The lowest level means finding that level of the foreign currency liquidity ratio that almost all foreign bank branches can observe. Even though regulations on foreign bank branches start at the lowest level, it will be important to introduce the same regulations on foreign bank branches as those applied to local banks. Second, regulations such as foreign currency liquidity ratios on foreign bank branches should be gradually strengthened, based on the outcome of regulations. Finally, regulations such as the foreign currency liquidity ratio on foreign bank branches should be adjusted to reach a certain level. But it will not be necessary to equalize the imposition of the level of regulations such as foreign currency liquidity ratio on foreign bank branches with that placed on domestic banks. This is because it, as in the case of forward position limit system, is necessary to acknowledge the special characteristics of foreign bank branches.

References

Ahn, Byung Chan (2008). "Capital Flows and Effects on Financial Markets in Korea: Developments and Policy Responses." *Financial Globalization and Emerging Market Capital Flows*. BIS Papers No. 44. September. pp. 307 and 317.

―― (2011). *Foreign Exchange Policies after the Global Financial Crisis (in Korean)*. Hannarae Publishing Co. May.

Aizenman, J., M. D. Chinn, & H. Ito (2008). "Assessing the emerging global financial architecture: measuring the trilemma's configurations over time." NBER working paper 14533. December.

Allen, Mark, et al. (2002). "A Balance Sheet Approach to Financial Crisis," IMF Working Paper.

Bank of Korea. *Annual Report*.

―― (2010). "Reinforcing Regulations on Foreign Currency Loan Use (in Korean)." Press Release. June 23.

―― (2010). *Foreign Exchange System and Foreign Exchange Market in Korea (in Korean)*. December.

BIS (2004). "Revisiting Foreign Exchange Reserve Adequacy." A Note for a Meeting of Governors. February 9.

BIS, IMF, OECD, & World Bank (2001). *Joint BIS-IMF-OECD-World Bank Statistics on External Debt*. November.

Cabinet of Korea. Enforcement Decree of the Foreign Exchange Transactions Act.

————. Enforcement Decree of the Banking Act.

Cline, William R. & John Williamson (2012). "Estimates of Fundamental Equilibrium Exchange Rates." Policy Brief 12–14. Peterson Institute for International Economics. May.

—— (2012). "Updated Estimates of Fundamental Equilibrium Exchange Rates." Policy Brief 12-23. Peterson Institute for International Economics. November.

Committee on the Global Financial System (2010). "Macroprudential Instruments and Frameworks: A Stocktaking of Issues and Experiences." CGFS Papers No. 38. BIS. May.

Council of the European Union (2013). "Financial transaction tax: Council agrees to enhanced cooperation." January 22.

Finance Ministers and Central Bank Governors of ASEAN+3 (2012). "The Joint Statement of the 15th ASEAN+3 Finance Ministers and Central Bank Governors' Meeting." Press Release. May 3.

Financial Services Commission. Regulation on Supervision of Banking Business.

Financial Supervisory Service (2009). "Domestic Banks' Long-term Funding Resources as of end-May 2009." Press Release. July 1.

—— (2011). "Domestic Financial Institutions' FX Soundness Ratio as of end-December 2010." Press Release. February 28.

—— (2013). "Domestic Banks' Foreign Currency Funding and Liquidity." Press Release. April 8.

Financial Times (2013). February 14.

Flood, R. & N. Marion (2002). "Holding International Reserves in an Era of High Capital Mobility." IMF Working Paper 02/62.

Garcia, Pablo S. & Claudio Soto (2004). "Large Hoarding of International Reserves: Are they worth it?" Central Bank of Chile Working Papers 299.

Greenspan, Alan. (2001). "Globalization." BIS Review 88.

—— (1999). "Currency Reserves and Debt, remarks before the World Bank Conference on Recent Trends in Reserve Management." Washington DC.

April 29.

G20 (2010). "The G20 Seoul Summit Leader's Declaration and the Seoul Summit Document." November 12.

Hau, H. & H. Rey (2006). "Exchange Rates, Equity Prices and Capital Flows." *Review of Financial Studies 19*.

Heritage Foundation and Wall Street Journal (2013). *2013 Index of Economic Freedom*. January.

IMF (1997). *World Economic Outlook* (Statistical Appendix). May.

—— (2003). *External Debt Statistics: Guide for Compilers and Users* (Final Draft, November 2001). October.

—— (2011). *Sixth edition of the Balance of Payments and International Investment Position Manual (BPM6)*. August.

—— (2011). *World Economic Outlook*. January.

Jeanne, O. & R. Rancière (2005). "The Optimal Level of International Reserves for Emerging Market Countries: Formulas and Applications." IMF Research Department.

Milken Institute (2010). *Capital Access Index 2009*. April.

Ministry of Strategy and Finance. Foreign Exchange Transaction Regulation.

Ministry of Strategy and Finance, Bank of Korea, etc. (2010). "New Macro-Prudential Measures to Mitigate Volatility of Capital Flows." Press Release. June 14.

—— (2010). "New Macro-Prudential Measures to Mitigate Volatility of Capital Flows, Q&A." Press Release. June 14.

Moody's Investors Service (2012). "Rating Action: Moody's Upgrades Korea to Aa3; outlook stable." August 27.

Moreno, Ramon (2011). "Policymaking from a "Macroprudential" Perspective in Emerging Market Economies." BIS Working Papers No. 336. January.

National Assembly of Korea. Foreign Exchange Transactions Act.

——. The Bank of Korea Act.

OECD (2012). *OECD Code of Liberalisation of Capital Movements*.

Oh, Jung Ryul (2010). "The Present Status of Foreign Exchange Liberalization

and Tasks Ahead in Korea." Bank of Korea. August 6.

Park, Yong-min & Gyeong Ho Kwon (2010). "Effects on the Foreign Exchange Sector of Shipbuilders' Exchange Rate Hedging (in Korean)." *Monthly Bulletin*. Bank of Korea. February.

Rosenberg, Michael R. (1996). *Currency Forecasting: A Guide to Fundamental and Technical Models of Exchange Rate Determination*. Irwin Professional Publishing.

U.S. Department of the Treasury (2012). "Report to Congress on International Economic and Exchange Rate Policies." November 27.

Wijinholds, J. O. & A. Kapteyn (2001). "Reserves Adequacy in Emerging Market Economies." IMF Working Paper WP/01/143. September.

World Bank (2002). *Global Development Finance*.

Yang, Yang Hyeon & Hye Lim Lee (2008). "An Analysis of the Attractions of Arbitrage Transactions and of Domestic Bond Investment by Foreigners and Korean Branches of Foreign Banks (in Korean)." *Monthly Bulletin*. Bank of Korea. August.

http://www.abs.gov.au

http://www.bcb.gov.br

http://www.bis.org

http://www.bok.or.kr

http://www.commerce.gov

http://www.fss.or.kr

http://www.imf.org

http://www.moleg.go.kr

http://www.oecd.org

http://www.treasury.gov

http://www.world-exchanges.org

Index